A Holy Hole In One

By

Zev Zahavish

© 2013 Zev Zahavish. All Rights Reserved
ISBN 978-0-615-88081-5

This is the view from the golf course, looking north to the Golan. The site is real, with Half Moon Bay Course Photoshopped in.

Contents

Introduction

One .... Grossinger's

Two .... Raising the Flag

Three .... Improving Your Lie

Four .... Culture

Five .... Enjoy Your Visit, but Please Don't Stay

Six............ October 6, 1973

Seven .... Hamadia

Eight .... US Electric

Nine .... The Community That Won't Admit It Exists

Ten........... The Dos

Eleven ...... CD Inc.

Twelve ...... The Fall

Thirteen ... Golf in Israel

Fourteen... A Holy Hole in One

Fifteen...... September 11, 2001

Sixteen ..... Passover 2002

Seventeen. Golf Heaven

Eighteen... Jordan River Golf

Nineteen... The Journey

Twenty ..... The End of the Beginning

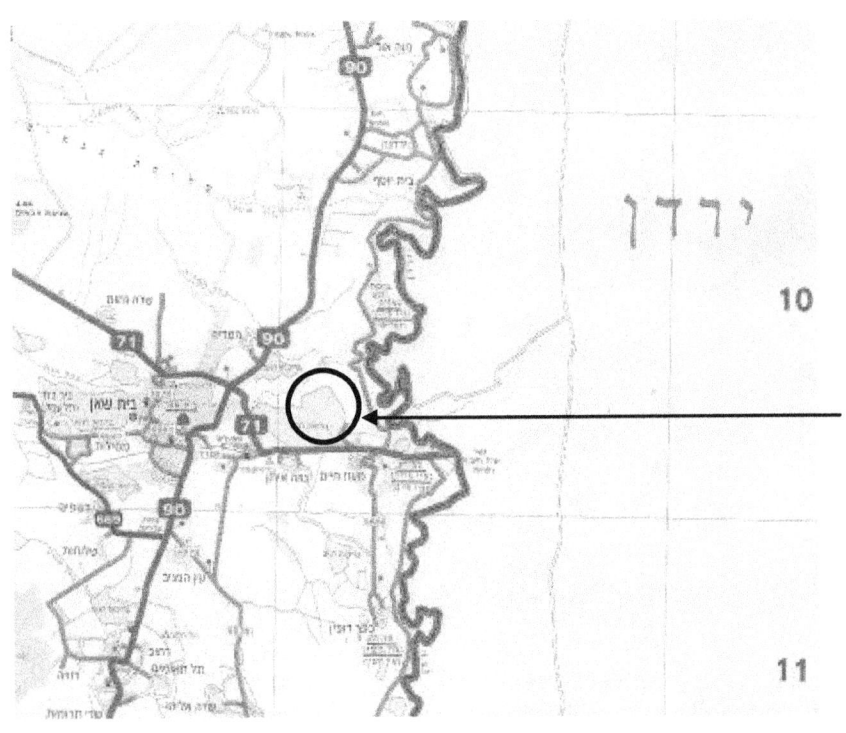

*The dark line is the Jordan River,
and the circled area is the site of the course.*

*A Whistling Streams view:
the Castles and the West Elk Wilderness Area.*

In loving memory of my grandma Yetta, my mom and dad, my sister Esta, and my friends Michael Columbus, David Dorfman, Michael Potoker, Jim Ozyp, Bill Yanaki, Marlene Icovetto Slusher, Rick Miller, and Ami Hamami.

עם ישראל חי

Introduction

This book has a purpose, and that is to raise funds to build the second, eighteen-hole golf course in Israel. Yes, that's right, in Israel—in the Bet Shean Valley, less than a mile from the Jordan River and three miles from the town of Bet Shean (which has a documented history going back 6,500 years). Most people think I am crazy when they hear I want to build a golf course in Israel. Well, this is a story of how I got there, and you can judge for yourself.

If you like golf, Israel, or travel, you should enjoy reading this story. Yes, I really did have a hole in one on the only eighteen-hole golf course in Israel. The Caesarea Golf Club still exists, and I am an ex-member who used to have his name on the wall. The problem is the course that I knew and loved has gone through a fancy Pete Dye redesign. The old course and the eighth hole, which was the sight of my hole in one, are gone.

The many friendships I made at Caesarea have enriched my life. The members come from all over the country and many colorful backgrounds. Bill Clinton is an honorary member. They are still waiting for him to show up and play.

If you haven't guessed by now, I have a passion for golf. At my age, no other sport gives me the exercise, pure enjoyment, and peace that golf does. I learned to play golf at the age of ten, and I have loved the game for fifty years. I have played the game in many amazingly beautiful places all over the world. Not all are in this story.

Golf heaven is the Monterey Bay area, as anyone who has played golf there will attest to. I was fortunate enough to live in Pacific Grove for a couple of years. It has a chapter in my story.

I believe in affordable golf, and that the game should be as close to free as possible for juniors. In Israel, they do a good job for the kids. Everyone else who wants to play there must pay the price. Israel has around twelve hundred golfers. It also has a short nine-hole course located not far from Tel Aviv and the Mediterranean Sea. Gaash is located between Hertzeliya and Netanya. I am told that Gaash is a very successful club, surpassing Caesarea. I have many friends who are former Caesarea members and now play there. Israel really needs an affordable golf course. I hope that the story you are about to read will fulfill its purpose, and Israel will soon have an affordable golf course.

This story is mostly about golf and my journey through life. I grew up in New York City and spent most of my life in one of the most beautiful places on the planet, in Gunnison County, Colorado. There are chapters about both here. The events all happened, and the places all exist. I have used nicknames and first names for the people mentioned in the story (except for historical figures), and all of them are real people.

My love for the land of Israel is not a simple thing to explain. My experiences span forty-four years and living through some of the worst periods in the country's history. Surviving a couple of wars and a civil insurrection was not easy to write about. I have seen the worst man can do to man.

The story you are about to read is not meant to make a political statement. My opinions and beliefs are my opinions and beliefs and are not meant to offend anyone.

My Hebrew name is Zev Zahavish. I grew up in a kosher home, where Grandma would light candles every Friday night. I was a bar-mitzvah boy in 1965, so I guess that qualifies me as a Jew. The funny thing is that I really don't believe in religion. If it works for you, great, but it has never worked for me. My feelings for Israel are not founded in religious belief. It's much more complicated.

Jerry Rubin once defined a yippie as a Jewish hippie, and I am guilty as charged. It might come as a shock to most Jewish Americans who live in and around the big cities, but anti-Semitism is a fact of life in the America I live in. My experience is proof. My story is not about religion.

My story has no steamy sex or romance. I don't believe in kiss and tell. Some major crushes have had an impact on my story. I have two daughters and a stepdaughter. They are grown-up and living their very busy, independent lives. They all have at least one college degree and have traveled outside of America.

Four years ago, I told my friends in Hamadia that I would not be back until I raised enough funds to build a golf course. The planning and permissions had been almost entirely completed, and it had taken only four years. I had dealt with dozens of potential investors and learned what frustration means. The only thing I lacked was funding. I have not given up on my dream. I had spent the last four years trying to forget and give up, but I just couldn't.

How do you explain a passion for golf to people who have no understanding of the sport? In the United States, over twenty million people will play golf in a year. In Israel, it will be around twelve hundred. I tried to define this passion to Israelis in an early business plan that I presented to the local government.

As I wrote in the plan, golf is nature. Golf is balance in all things. Golf is focus. Golf is beauty. Golf is a long walk. Golf is a seventy-plus-billion-dollar industry in America. Golf is a way of life. Golf is being polite. Golf is playing by the rules. Golf is emotion. Golf is patience and humility. Golf is joy. Golf is hope. Golf is peace.

There are thousands of golf communities across the United States but only one in Israel. It is one of the most affluent communities in Israel, developed by the Rothchilde family of Switzerland. Caesarea was originally an old Roman resort town, and you can walk through its ruins today. Situated on the Mediterranean Sea, its sunsets can be colorful.

The Caesarea golf community is varied, as it has many expatriates from around the world who play there. In many ways, having so many different cultures in the same club makes for great entertainment and challenging communication. The original power-elite of the club was South African. There are lots of Israeli members, but the truth is that most Israelis have a hard time with golf.

Playing golf in Israel is an adventure, and you never know what you might see or whom you might meet on the golf course. Diplomats play there, and international incidents can happen. One day I witnessed an altercation that I worried would come to blows.

Israelis have a problem with patience, and good golf etiquette is a mystery there. One day I was playing with Simon and Yair, who are good Israeli golfers. They liked to play fast, regardless of the course conditions. They would often hit into the group ahead, hoping the group would let them pass and often causing problems. On this day, the poor South Koreans in front of us had nowhere to go, as the course was backed up. We were having a slow round on the seventeenth tee when Yair snapped. Yair could not wait any longer and hit his drive right into the group ahead, causing the South Koreans to start yelling at him. He was not happy with the group's slow play, so he yelled and cursed back. Well, the Koreans decided to drive back to the tee box and confront Yair—a big mistake, in my opinion. Yair was a missile salesman, a former gunship squadron commander, a pilot, and ex-air force colonel. In good shape and a very arrogant person at times, Yair got right into the Koreans' faces. When one Korean waved his finger in front of Yair's face, I thought someone would have to call 9-1-1. Simon eventually got Yair under control, and no physical damage was done.

I had come to Israel to reinvent myself; I was studying the language and playing a lot of golf. I had gone through a horrible divorce and was just happy to be in Israel. I have a long history in Israel, and, after living through the Black War, I thought I had lived through the worst times Israel could offer. The second intifada would rival my experience in horror.

I have been playing golf for over fifty years. I learned at the age of ten on a golf course that no longer exists. Golf is a difficult and frustrating game to learn. The more you play, the better you should get. As a kid, I could hit a nine iron really well and straight. Being consistent is the hardest part of learning the game. Everyone who plays golf eventually hits a great shot. The feeling of satisfaction in hitting a great shot gives you hope for the next one. A perfect shot is rare but always memorable.

A hole in one is a moment of golf perfection. Once achieved, it is something you always remember. For one swing, you have achieved the perfect result and put the ball in the hole from a decent distance away. Some people say a hole in one is all luck. I have been lucky enough to make three holes in one. The most memorable and meaningful one came in Caesarea during a competition. Holes in one are rare in Israel too, but no one could remember one that was made in competition.

I fell deeper in love with the game of golf as a result. As I kept playing golf in Israel, I wished even more that it would have more than one eighteen-hole golf course. I feel Israel could support ten golf courses. I have met a few people who agree but as of today have not been successful in bringing more golf to Israel. It is not an easy thing to make happen.

I tried to think of something I would enjoy working at in Israel. I still had many friends living in Hamadia, a place where I once lived and worked. The problem was that Hamadia is not the community it once was. It was on the verge of bankruptcy and no longer guaranteed its residents employment. The kibbutz way of life was over, and everyone now living there has to pay his or her own expenses for everything.

Hamadia does have thousands of acres being leased out instead of worked. It has a new national park on one of its borders. Building a golf course around the park seemed to be a perfect fit. The more I thought about it, the more it made sense. Golf has a positive impact in many economic ways. The kibbutz sure could have used an economic boost.

The town of Bet Shean is located about two miles away from Hamadia. It has ancient ruins that go back 6,500 years. Hundreds of thousands of tourists visit each year, but no one spends the night. The town recently got its first hotel. A golf development in the area would be a major asset. It would enhance the quality of life and generate more tourism. It's a win-win proposition. And it was not difficult to find support for the project. The problem was, who was going to pay for its construction? Hamadia was a mess financially, and the local government was in almost as bad shape. It would be up to me to find the funds for a golf-course construction.

Finding a partner for the project became more difficult than I ever imagined. When you have a vision of a project that will benefit thousands of people and has a relatively small cost, you don't envision failure. After all, I wasn't reinventing the wheel; the business model was proven.

This book tells the story of my journey through life and how I came to be in a position to build a golf course in Israel. It is my hope that enough people will see the benefit in bringing more golf to Israel and that enough people can make a difference.

The joy and peace I have come to know playing the game of golf has been an important part of my life. Few things in my life have given me more happiness. I would like to share that happiness in a part of the world that sorely needs it.

Israel has not known a day of peace since its founding in 1948. The state of Israel lives. It is one place in the world where a person with a Jewish last name is not a problem. It was created in the aftermath of the Holocaust. It became a place where Jews could go home and not be evicted because of their religion. The fact it exists is a miracle, and it is ever-evolving and changing.

Israel is no longer the poor socialist state it was at the time of the Six-Day War. The pioneers who are still alive are old and in the way. The problem of the pioneers is now the problem of the next generation. The problem is neighbors who want to wipe you from the face of the earth. How many generations will it take to solve the problem? It's hard to say, but most people I know there pray for peace.

Today Israel is a world-class tourist destination, and its citizens enjoy a higher standard of living than their neighbors. Its economy is diverse, from high-tech to state-of-the-art agriculture. Israel is probably the most secure country in the world. Its security industry is diverse, and it is a world leader in providing systems. Its people yearn for peace but prepare for war. Civilized history goes a long way back, and, of course, religion was born there.

Its people come in all colors and from every culture. Some had no other option, as many Arab states expelled Jews when Israel was founded. It has seen a large immigration from Russia after the fall of Communism. Russian immigration has made Israel a much stronger country. Today Israeli society is vibrant and incredibly strong. Its citizens depend on one another for survival, and every citizen is responsible. Few citizens in the world have the responsibility of an Israeli.

I hope the story you are about to read gives you a greater understanding of golf and Israel. A dream is worth fighting for, so they say. Building golf in Israel is a noble goal. By purchasing and reading this book, you are trying to make a difference, and for that I thank you.

If you enjoy this story, tell a friend to buy the book. If you hate it and want to tell me how crazy I am, I would love to hear from you all. Contact me at my website: www.holyholeinone.org.

One

Grossinger's

The hills of Hollis are located in New York City in the borough of Queens. The people who live in the neighborhood call it Hollis Hills, even though the zip code goes to the Queens Village post office. It is and was one of the nicer neighborhoods in New York City. It is not the kind of neighborhood you might think exists there.

Hollis Hills has two large parks—Alley Pond and Cunningham—on its borders. It has a bicycle path that connects them. The Grand Central Parkway is also one of the borders. When the Throgs Neck Bridge and the Clearview

Expressway were built and the Grand Central expanded by two lanes, it destroyed hundreds of acres of parkland. Green Fields and Pea Pond no longer exist, but I have many fond childhood memories of both places. Pea Pond was just a few blocks from my house. People used to ice-skate and fish in its water. The water has been gone for fifty years, and you can't even call the place a mud-hole today.

Hollis Hills is a neighborhood of single-family homes, with everyone having a front- and backyard. The streets are mostly numbered; my house was on Eighty-Second Avenue, and I loved growing up there.

The neighborhood has three churches, two of which have schools. When I lived there, the neighborhood was mostly Jewish, and we were members of the Hollis Hills Jewish Center until I was thirteen. My mom and dad were not religious at all and never attended services, even on the high holidays. They kept a kosher home, because my grandma lived with us.

I grew up in a house that had a mom and dad and two older sisters. My oldest sister, Esta, was thirteen years old when I was born, and my oldest memory of her was her going off to college. Sandy was only six years older and more of a friend. My maternal grandmother also lived with us. She was the only grandparent alive when I was born.

My grandma was my favorite person and best friend. She made the most outrageous challah bread every Friday, and, of course, I could not wait to get my grubby little paws on it.

Grandma came from a religious family, and she said she grew up in the town of Buckashevitz in Austria. I once tried to find the place, but no one knew the place existed. I always thought it was in or near Vienna, but, in his biography, one of her brothers said he grew up in the Carpathian Mountains. The same brother would help build the Jewish Center of the Hamptons. Another brother helped build the first temple in Miami Beach, on Lincoln Road. Grandma, not my mom and dad, made me go to temple on the holidays.

My mom never showed any real interest in me, but my dad loved me. He worked a lot, though, and was very successful. I had older parents; my mom gave birth to me in her forties, and my dad was in his fifties. My dad died when I was eleven years old. My mom once visited my place in Colorado, and, after a few belts of scotch at a neighbor's house, told the story of how she had wanted an abortion, thinking she was too old to have another child. My dad, being the great salesman that he was, told my mom that he would hire a nurse to do all the dirty work, and so I came into being.

I do remember a couple of my nurses and one in particular. Her name was Rochelle, and she came from Quebec and tried to teach me French. Supposedly I spoke more French than English at one time. I have a number of French friends, and I can understand a little bit of the language today. When I speak, I butcher it pretty badly. When I go to France, and I ask people if they speak English, of course they answer no. So I go into my French spiel, and, voilà, they speak English like champs. Mary, my first nurse, would eventually get fired for teaching me to pray to Jesus before I went to sleep.

My grade-school education took place at Public School 188, across the turnpike and about six blocks from my house. It had a fenced school yard. I spent many, many hours playing there. We would play speedball (a version of stickball), touch football, and, of course, basketball. One of the fences ran along the backyards of about twelve houses. Almost all the houses were OK with us retrieving a ball. One, the "old lady's house", however, was game over—just like in the movie *The Sandlot*, except the dog was a Doberman, not a cuddly Saint Bernard. Her backyard was also fenced tighter than Fort Knox, and I don't know anyone who ever got a ball back out of there. She would come out and yell at us for looking in her yard. I have no idea what she did with the hundreds of Pensie Pinkies and Spalding rubber balls that ended up in her yard through the years. I have a feeling she just threw them away.

I love hoops, or basketball, and 188 had two baskets but not a full court. We would play for hours there, but eventually, as we grew older, we moved several blocks north to Public School 205 in the Windsor Park neighborhood, which was mostly apartment buildings. PS 205 had a full court, but it was a lot busier, and sometimes we had to challenge to get on it.

My first exposure to the game of golf came at Grossinger's resort in the Catskill Mountains near Liberty, New York. Grossinger's was part of the Borscht Belt, a bunch of resorts catering to mostly Jewish clientele. Browns, Concord, Kutsher's, Stevensville, Neville, Pines, and the Laurels were some of the other resorts that made up the belt. Only Kutsher's, I believe, is around today. The Grossinger's and Concord golf courses also remain in operation today.

My first recollection of a family vacation happened at Grossinger's. It sure was a fun place for a little kid. It had a huge Olympic-sized pool with different elevations of diving boards and a thirty-meter-high platform. One time I jumped off the thirty-meter platform, and what I remember is that I didn't want to do it again. The pool had a giant patio that served lunch, and I remember great burgers. Next to the patio were the shuffleboard and volleyball courts. The resort also had a large indoor pool and workout rooms downstairs.

I don't know if anyone will remember this, but Grossinger's would host the annual world barrel-jumping championship on its large ice-skating rink. ABC's *Wide World of Sports* would cover it, and I believe the champion was Irving Jaffe, who held the world record of twenty-four barrels.

Lou Goldstein was the resort's social director, and he was king of the game Simon Says. Every day, usually at poolside, a mob of people would try to hang with Lou. Try as they might, nobody could last long in the game. Lou could make people do what they didn't want to do. I think my mom kind of liked Lou—he was a bit of a ladies' man. It was sure fun to watch.

Grossinger's also had top-name entertainment on the weekends. It had its showroom, and I remember one show in particular. Leslie Uggams was the headliner, and the Half Brothers were the warm-up act. They juggled pretty much everything: balls, hoops, torches, and bowling pins. Anyway, they asked for a volunteer from the audience; I raised my hand, and they picked me. When I got to the stage, one of the brothers whispered in my ear, "When my brother asks where you're from, say 'Boise, Idaho.'" I nodded, and we headed to center stage. The brother asked, and I said, "Boise, Idaho," and got a big laugh. They put a funky top hat on my head, a plastic-wrapped cigar in my mouth, and a small paperback book in my hand to hold. They walked about fifteen yards from each other, with me in the middle. They started playing catch with bowling pins, and the next thing I knew, the book, the hat, and the cigar were all gone. Big applause; I was a hit. I got back to my seat, and my mom was giving me a look. She was angry that I had said I was from Boise, Idaho. When she asked me why I said that, I told her the guy told me to say that. She just looked away. I don't think she believed me, but she let it go.

The first time I ever walked a golf course was to watch Sam Snead put on an exhibition match at Grossinger's. I remember the beauty of the course and the huge distance Sam could hit the ball off the tee. I don't remember who the other pro was, but he wasn't even close to Sam's distance. I remember the fun of just walking on the beautiful grass.

Grossinger's closed as a resort in the late seventies. The three nine-hole courses were still open when I finally played the course ten years ago. It was just as beautiful as I remembered from my childhood. It is sad that the resort is gone. My best childhood memories of my family being together and having fun were at Grossinger's.

Two
Raising the Flag

My dad was my hero. He loved sports, though I doubt he played much when he was a kid. He met my mom on a boat trip on the Hudson River. My dad had a tough life growing up—not like his son. He never got to high school, because he had to work to support his family. He worked for Western Union as a kid and eventually wound up selling radios for a Brooklyn wholesaler. In my father's scrapbook, he had articles from Yiddish newspapers, so I guess he sold a few radios. Anyway, one day he called in sick and went to a

Brooklyn Dodgers game at Ebbets Field. Someone spotted him there, word got back to the boss, and the next day he was fired.

When I asked my dad if he was ever in the army, he chuckled and said he was in the Salvation Army. It was 1942, and my dad would go to Washington, DC, to try and get radio contracts from the military. He would eventually get some contracts and go on to start his own company. He represented factories such as Motorola, Morse Electronics, Jacobsen, and Lakewood Engineering. He sold their products to America's largest retailers at the time.

In 1959, my dad bought season tickets to watch the New York Giants. My dad's best friend lived in the neighborhood and also had tickets. We would all go to the home games together. I loved and anticipated going to each game with my dad. Of course I knew all the players and remember most of them now, as the Giants were good and played in a lot of championships. We sat in section thirty-six in the upper deck of old Yankee Stadium, and occasionally I got to bring a friend. One guy who sat above us would have been fit for a part in *The Godfather.* He would constantly yell, "Gifford under the goalpost," whenever the Giants got into the red zone. I was in the stands when Bednarik hit the Giff, and I never heard so many people go so quiet.

The only vacations that I would get to go on would be to Grossinger's, but in 1961, we all flew to Florida and stayed at the Hollywood Beach Hotel. It was the first time I got to sleep next to the ocean.

From 1960 through 1968, I would spend every summer at camp. I was eight years old when I first went to camp; Sandy had been going for as long as I could remember. I went to a camp named Indian Trails in Milford, Pennsylvania, in the Pocono Mountains. It was a small camp with a lake, and it was there that I learned to swim. They also had sailboats, and I learned to sail. We went on overnight camping trips, and that was my first experience sleeping outdoors. I could have done without the ghost stories, but overnights were a lot of fun. My first two summers of camp were spent at Indian Trails, and, aside from the ukulele lessons, I have nothing but wonderful memories.

The Hollywood Beach Hotel was where my dad met "Tex" Amdur and heard about "the haven of health and happiness." Uncle Tex had a unique voice that sounded a lot like Froggy the Gremlin that was a sidekick on *Andy's Gang*, a Saturday morning kids' show. Hosted by Andy Devine and the puppet frog, Andy would ask the kids to shout, "Plunk your magic twanger, Froggy," and then the frog would appear and greet us with the famous line, "Hi ya, kids. Hi ya. Hi ya." Uncle Tex was a school principal in Brooklyn and owned and operated Camp Roosevelt, located off Sacket Lake, about ten miles from the town of Monticello, New York. Roosevelt was much bigger and more sports-oriented than Indian Trails. The flagpole ceremony every morning and evening had a few hundred kids. It was also kind of religious; we had to give a prayer of thanks before every meal and attend a Saturday service. Its most famous ex-camper was probably Ralph Lauren. Roosevelt was where I learned to play golf.

Roosevelt had a cage and a short range. The cage and range would be where my first attempts at hitting a golf ball took place. They would take us around the lake to the Laurels Hotel to play on a real course. The Laurels and the nine-hole course are gone today. I would go play there every chance I was allowed. Not only was it a way out of camp life, but also

I enjoyed hitting the ball and walking around the pretty countryside.

The Laurels golf course was not difficult, but it had a couple of long holes. It was definitely pretty enough. Usually few people were on the course, so we could make all the mistakes we wanted without slowing anyone down.

My first year at camp, I had a couple of friends from PS 188, so I adjusted well to my new camp. Activities were basketball, softball, baseball, tennis, football, horseback riding, hiking, swimming, waterskiing, and boating (no sailboats). Girls went to my camp as well, so we had socials, and we would go on raids, which required great stealth to get to the girls' side of camp. If you got caught out of your bunk (cabin), you were docked free play or a movie. Years later, I returned to visit one of my nephews and found him sitting docked at Bunk One. Free play was the best, because you could do anything you wanted anywhere at camp. We had many special events, such as plays, movies, Carnival, and the Olympics.

Back in the day, the New York Knickerbockers would send their players to camps for clinics and fun. I got to meet Butch Komives and Willis Reed once when they gave a clinic. Of course the Knicks traded Komives and Walt Bellamy for Dave Debushere, and the Knicks stopped coming to visit. I got to play at the old Madison Square Garden. Yep, one year the Knicks invited us to play at halftime of their game and the high school game before theirs. I don't remember scoring or playing for that long, but a younger kid asked me for my autograph. It was an experience to remember.

The camp had a secret, or honor, society called Blue Dragon. The best and only good thing they did was to have an end-of-camp cookout and bonfire. You had to get elected by the campers in the society. It would be some years, but eventually I got to eat an extra barbecue.

We would have inter-camp competitions almost every week. We would compete against other camps, such as Sequoia, Olympus, Tyler Hill, and Anawana. I had quite a few neighborhood friends who went to Tyler Hill, and it was always fun to beat them. We at Roosevelt usually always won.

The climax of camp was the color war, when the camp would be divided into two teams: blue and gray. We would compete in all sports, as well as acting and singing. One song was sung year after year, and I still remember the words. "In Strong Array" was set to the music of the French national anthem, "Le Marseilles."

One year they added golf to the competition. A flag was set up on the range, and the idea was to hit the target that was around ninety yards away. The closer you were to the flag, the more points you were awarded. Most kids missed the target, but all three of my shots went in, and two were close to the pin. I scored almost as many points as the entire other team had, and my team easily won. I was awarded flag-of-the-day honors and called out to the flagpole to lower the flag.

My birthday is in August, so I spent a lot of birthdays in camp. At Roosevelt, if you had a birthday during camp, you got to raise the flag at morning assembly. I may not have had birthday parties and presents, but I did get to raise the flag for more than a few summers on my birthday.

I will always be grateful to my mom and dad for sending me to camp. Some kids didn't like it; some didn't want to leave home for two months. I thrived in camp and was always sad to go home and go back to school.

One summer I came home from camp to find my dad in the hospital. I was told it was nothing serious, and that he would be home soon. A few months later, my dad would die from lung cancer.
After my dad's death, life got harder. Sandy was going off to Cornell, and I was stuck with Mom and Grandma at home. It took a couple of years to accept my dad's death. I would dream he was still alive, and that we still did fun things.

After my dad died, my mom continued to send me to camp. My mom would ship me off to camp and then travel the world with Sandy. They traveled in style, and I have to admit I was jealous when I saw the pictures and heard their stories. I vowed to myself I would travel and see the world one day.

Three

Improving Your Lie

I was a good student in grade school, but after my dad died, I lost interest. I would do enough to get by, but I never challenged myself or put much effort into school. Junior High School 109 was located in Queens Village and was totally different from my grade school. I had to take a bus to get there and home, because it was five miles away.

From day one there, I knew school would be different. I actually didn't get to go to school on the first day because of a parent protest against forced school integration. Queens

Village and Hollis Hills were all-white back then. A new law was introduced to integrate all-white schools, and the community of Queens Village was not happy about it. After a week, the protest died out, and I went to school.

My mom and her family were bigots, and they didn't get along well with people who weren't Jewish. I never felt that I was better than anyone because of my race or religion. At my junior high school, JHS109, I learned that people didn't like me because of my very Jewish last name. They called me names, and I called them names. I got along better with the black kids, and they never called me names. I liked to play basketball, and maybe that was why. When I invited a black kid to visit my house, my mom was not happy about it and told me not to do it again.

I never got into fights or had any trouble, except one time. I was walking home from grade school when a kid from the Catholic school decided to pick on me. (I had many routes to and from school, and one was walking past the Catholic school.) The kid was twice my size and wound up giving me a black eye. When I got home, my mom was upset. We had to go visit the nun's house to show them what one of their students had done. I never understood the purpose, because I didn't know the kid's name, but I think my mom felt better after her visit with the nuns.

I attended and graduated from Martin Van Buren High School. With over four thousand students and only three grades, it was more like a factory than a school. There were so many students that we could not all go to school at the same time. My sophomore year I went to school at half past noon and finished after five o'clock. My junior year, I went from nine to three, and my senior year, from half past seven in the morning to half past noon. My graduating class was made up of 1,635 students, and I finished in the top 25 percent. My graduation was held in Forest Park. I remember four hundred kids in my gym class. We never had a prom, because there were too many kids, and the school had police patrolling the corridors.

We didn't have a football team, but we did have a basketball team. As if we didn't have enough students, our basketball coach used to recruit players from outside the district. We had the best team in the borough of Queens. Boys High had the best team in the city. At the time, Boys and DeWitt Clinton would knock us off in the city championships. In Israel, I used to joke with my friends who enjoyed watching Israeli professional basketball that my high-school team was more fun to watch and had more talent. We had a great team, but unfortunately our star player was shot and arrested in a grocery store holdup and would never play at the next level.

My friends from the neighborhood and I were not good enough to play for Van Buren. We did play for Hollis Hills Jewish Center in the Jewish-center league. Yes, there was a Jewish-center league, and we would play teams from Bell Park, Hillcrest, Bellrose, Bayside, and Flushing. We won more than we lost, but, of course, we never played before a crowd. Flushing had the best team; they had two players who were black, and, worse, they were tall and strong and could actually jump. I am sure they weren't Jewish. I am not sure if the Jewish-center league exists today, but I doubt it.

In the late sixties, when I went to high school, the times were definitely changing. The war in Vietnam was a big deal, and no one I knew from the neighborhood wanted to go or actually went. We did have two fatalities from the neighborhood because of the Vietnam War. Two of the four students killed at the Kent State antiwar protest were from Hollis Hills. They were girls who did nothing wrong but were in the wrong place at the wrong time—they certainly didn't deserve to die. The brother of my good friend Hoofy was there at the time, and I remember watching his homemade movie of the event. The families of the victims, to my best recollection, never received justice, because none of the Ohio National Guardsmen who fired into the crowd that day were ever brought to trial.

Drugs, such as LSD, quaaludes, speed, and pot, were around when I was in high school, but I never tried them then. In college they were a big deal, and, yes, I attended many wild parties. These days I prefer a joint to a drink, and I am not much of a partier.

We held student protests against the war in Vietnam in high school, and it was a good way to get out of classes. We would also go to demonstrations in Manhattan's Central Park. The best demonstrations were down in Washington, DC, during my college years. Hundreds of thousands of kids would show, and we would camp out on the mall, listen to great music, and make love.

I went to Baruch College in Manhattan, and the only reason I went was to avoid being drafted into the army. After my first year of college, the government decided it would hold a lottery to determine who would be drafted. There were so many people born in 1952 that they couldn't draft us all. Your birthday determined your draft number, and my lucky number was 285. They took only numbers of a hundred and below. A few friends with low numbers had to go to shrinks to certify that they were mentally unstable or gay. Anyway, none of my childhood friends went into the army. Those born in 1952 were the last to be drafted and have to serve. It didn't matter if you studied for ten years; if you had a low number, you had to serve. When the Vietnam War ended, the army became all volunteer.

In 1968, while I was in summer camp, my mother and Sandy were on one of their world tours. They traveled through Europe, and this year the itinerary included Israel. They were flying from Tel Aviv to Eilat, the Israeli town on the Red Sea. The domestic airport in Tel Aviv is right next to an airforce base. All the flight announcements were in Hebrew, and, since neither my mom nor Sandy spoke or understood Hebrew at the time, they asked a group of soldiers who were standing around if anyone spoke English. This was how Sandy met the love of her life. Two weeks later, she was engaged to be married to one of the soldiers.

In December of 1968, I made my first journey to Israel to attend her wedding. I traveled with my grandma, and I remember having to lug a bunch of Sandy's favorite albums. The trip was incredibly long. We had a five-hour layover in Paris, and, because of a bad experience, Grandma had been flying to Miami (she got off the plane in Tampa and did not get back on in time); she would not get off the plane in Paris. The trip took twenty hours.

The wedding took place at the Palace Hotel in Netanya. My brother-in-law Nachum spent a whole ten dollars on the wedding ring. I know, because I was with him when he bought it. Sandy was a recent Cornell graduate and came from substance. The guy she was marrying had nothing and was committed to the air force for two more years. He wasn't even a pilot. I just didn't get it. They have been happily married now for forty-four years, have two wonderful sons, and are expecting their fourth grandchild in a few months. They are still in love. What do I know?

The highlight of the first trip was going to the Western Wall in the old city of Jerusalem. Grandma was religious, and I expected it to be big, emotional experience for her—or at least she would pray at the wall. Nope—Grandma fooled me. She pulled up a chair next to the curtain (Orthodox Jewish men and women do not pray together, and the curtain divides male and female praying areas at the wall) and just stared at the men praying at the wall. When I asked her what she thought about it afterward, she said, "It was no big deal."

The summer of 1969 was the summer of love, the summer of Woodstock. Camp Roosevelt was not that far from Woodstock, but I would attend neither that summer. My first summer not in camp would be spent at the Accadia Hotel in Hertzeliya. My sister lived in Netanya, but at the time, there was no hotel nice enough for my mom there.

In 1969, Israel was a totally different country than it is today. It was a very poor country back then. Not many people owned cars, and there was no television. Some people had them, but the only programming was one channel that came from Jordan. The people were still giddy from their tremendous victory in the Six-Day War. They felt invincible, even though they still had troubles.

There were daily attacks in Sinai, and there were almost daily attacks in the place I now call my home in Israel, in the Bet Shean Valley. Those places were far removed from the population centers, and most people were not concerned with the attacks. Black September was when King Hussein forced the PLO out of Jordan and stopped the attacks in the Bet Shean Valley, for the most part. The war of attrition in Sinai would continue for a few years.

The Accadia Hotel is a great place located on the Mediterranean Sea. Aside from having a great beach, it has a great pool. Back then, Israelis could pay a day rate and hang out at the pool. The hotel had one of the few tennis courts in the country, and I taught my brother-in-law the game. He could barely hit the ball, but eventually he got better and better, to the point where he now plays the game much better than I do. I had a girlfriend from Geneva, Switzerland, whom I liked a lot. She spent a couple of weeks at the hotel. I would look her up a few years later, and we had a great dinner at the Café De Paris in Geneva.

Hertzeliya was like all of Israel and was a lot less developed than it is today. My sister Sandy had a white Mustang convertible shipped from the States, so we traveled in style. Sandy had gone to Ulpan Akiva (a Hebrew school in Netanya) and could speak some Hebrew. We traveled all over the northern part of Israel and visited many different places.

My favorite place was a park not far from the town of Bet Shean and located between the Nir David and Bet Alpha kibbutzim. Gan Hashlosha, or Sachne, has waterfalls and swimming holes with lots of green grass to stretch out on. We visited a few times that summer, and it was a great change from the beach.

My sister and brother-in-law would eventually leave Israel in 1972. That summer by the sea was an amazing experience, and I learned an appreciation for the beauty that is Israel.

I played golf as much as I could during my school years. A lot of my friends' parents belonged to country clubs, and my friends knew how to play golf. My parents belonged to Muttontown, near C.W. Post College. I never played there, and after my dad's death, we were no longer members. My mom tried to learn the sport but had a hard time with it.

My friends and I would mostly play the city courses near our neighborhood. We would take a couple of buses to play at Kissena Park. Douglaston was a hilly, fun course that had too many par threes. It was closest to my neighborhood, but we still needed a lift to get there. The same with Clearview—it was the prettiest of the three, and it has a view of Long Island Sound and the Throgs Neck Bridge. A reserved tee time was a thing of the future, and waiting was a fact on city courses. Occasionally we would take a bus to Kissena before dawn, and we still had to wait.

My oldest sister Esta lived in Plainview, which is very close to Bethpage State Park. It has five nice courses and one extremely difficult course. The Black course has been the site of two US Opens and has recently hosted a tour event. My mom would drop us off and pick us up on occasion. We would play the course with the shortest wait time. The wait time was always a lot shorter than what we had to deal with on a city course.

I have played a lot of different courses on Long Island. My favorite is the Lake Success golf club. The town of Lake Success owns it, and, if you are a resident, you can play there. It has a limited number of nonresident memberships. My old friend Big Ed lives in the neighboring town of New Hyde Park. He spent fifteen years on the waiting list before finally succeeding in becoming a member. Lake Success is a fair and well-maintained course.

My friends and I had many great times playing golf as kids. For me it was an escape to a parklike setting. Our etiquette may not have been the best, and we probably didn't obey all the rules, but we sure had fun. One thing I liked to do back then was noodle the ball. The grass on the city courses wasn't the best, and you could get some bad lies in the fairway. Sometimes I would twist the grass into a tee and put my ball on top, and my friends would give me a hard time. They claimed I was cheating, but who was I was cheating? We weren't in a competition, and we certainly weren't playing for money. We were not pros; we were kids out to have fun. Golf is not an easy game. I developed my appreciation for golf as a kid. Today I follow the rules out of respect for the game. I do still have friends in Israel who play no bad lies, just as I did as a kid when I would improve my lie. They are my kind of people.

Four

Culture

*This is my favorite clubhouse in Oudenarde, Belgium.
Not only does it have a bar but also a prayer chapel.*

I spent my last summer at Camp Roosevelt working as a counselor. Being a counselor was not as much fun as being a camper. I did get a day off every week and would usually sneak into Grossinger's or the Concord and hang out at the pool. I remember having to register for the draft in the city on one day off and being classified twos.

In retrospect, I wish I had taken college more seriously. I applied only to one college in the city and was accepted. Baruch College is the business school of the City University of New York. I still lived at home, and the commute to get there was a nightmare. My house was only twelve miles from the city, but it would take at least an hour—sometimes two hours—to get there. It didn't matter whether you drove or took a
bus and a subway. The college was basically an office building, had no campus, and I hated it.

I was enrolled in classes, but after the first month, I decided to get a job in Lake Success, not far from home. I pretended to go to school but would work. I got my driver's license at eighteen, as I felt no need to drive a car in high school. The next two summers I would travel in Europe for the first time.

For 165 dollars, you could fly round-trip to Europe. It was a lot cheaper than flying to the West Coast. My first trip my mom bought me a car, a Peugeot 504, and I picked it up in London. It was a neat little car, and I gave it the name Pierre. Driving on the wrong side of the road was an adventure. We traveled to York in the north of England. York was a university town and had a quaint market. I was traveling with a college friend, and we stayed with his friends at the university.

We split up in the south of France, and my friend went on to Spain, and I headed to Greece. My first trip to Europe felt mystical—everything was a revelation. Just to be out of America felt good, and I was seeing new cultures in real life.

My first trip of any length on a boat was on a ferry crossing the English Channel. It was rough, and I was feeling bad, so I started drinking Cognac and felt better. My first trip to

France was memorable and enjoyable. The people I met were no more arrogant than New Yorkers or Texans. It seemed to me that once I made an attempt at their language, people would try to help me out. I camped in the Bois de Boulogne in Paris, hitting the Louvre, Versailles, and the Champs. I found Paris to be a world-class city with a great culture.

We drove south, and, the farther south we went, the prettier it got. Eventually we got to the Cote D' Azur on the Mediterranean Sea. We set up camp in Cagnes su Mer, about five miles west of Nice. We would hit the beaches of Cannes, Antibes, and Jean les Pan. The beach at Nice was all rocks, and I would say Cannes' beach was my favorite.

I split from my college buddy and arrived in Italy. I wasn't in *Italia* long when a motorcycle policeman stopped me. He yelled at me for at least fifteen minutes straight. I tried to interrupt him multiple times, but he would just yell louder. I learned Spanish in high school, and Italian has a lot of words in common with Spanish. What I could figure out was that I had crossed a solid, white line on the road, and that was like our stop sign, but without an *alto* sign, I didn't know to stop. Anyway, he finally shut up and looked at me. I asked him nicely if he spoke English. He just rolled his eyes, threw his hands in the air, and then got back on his motorcycle and drove away.

I visited Genoa, Parma, Venice, Pisa, Firenze, Bologna, Roma, Naples, Pompeii, and Brindisi. Camping outside Venice, I met more mosquitoes in one place than I thought possible. In Parma I found a great restaurant. Firenze was magical, and I had the campground figured out: I was never around when the guy came to collect the money.

On my first trip to Europe I spent more than five dollars a day because of gas, but on my second trip, I spent a lot less money. The Pitti Palace is my kind of palace. I was lucky enough to time my visit with Firenze's summer festival. I accidentally crashed a wedding on my way to visit Michelangelo's statue of David. Firenze gets my vote as best town in Italia.

I saw my first and only rock concert in Bologna. The bill was Emerson Lake & Palmer with the J. Geils Band. It was open seating at the football stadium, and we got there a little early and found seats fairly close. It kind of shocked me that the fence that surrounded the field was topped with barbed wire. The people who were sitting above us would pelt us with garbage. After a while, we just moved out of the line of fire. It wasn't that great a concert.

I don't know how Pierre and I survived *Roma*. Back in 1971, Roma had few traffic lights. (Years later, my oldest daughter Lauren would study a semester in Roma, and when I visited then, I noticed a lot more traffic lights.) Driving takes a certain bit of courage in Italia. In Naples I broke down and cried during the ultimate traffic nightmare. A minor fender bender turned into at least thirty minutes of two people arguing over whose fault it was. The blaring horns were amazing, and, of course, I had no escape.

Back then the south of Italia was poorer than the north, but the people were warm everywhere. Italia is my favorite country in Europe: the best food, culture, and art, and, of course, the hottest ladies.

I traveled with a Frisbee in those days, and while waiting for the ferry to Corfu, I drew quite a crowd. I don't think they had seen many Frisbees in Brindisi. Corfu is one of the prettiest islands I would ever visit. Back then, Ermonos Bay was pristine, and its only development was a house and a taverna. Ermonos was to be my base on Corfu.

There was a small town called Vatos on the other side of the hill. In the summer of 1971, lots of hippies from all over the world camped down a trail on the beach not far from Vatos. I became famous for wiping out a moped in the center of town. That day I was headed to Glyfada, and I thankfully met someone who patched me up. I also ran into someone from the neighborhood, proving it is indeed a small world.

I thought Ermonos was the prettiest spot I would ever see in the world. The water had more color than the sky. They were building a resort into the hillside, and I knew it would all change. Andreas and his family were the only residents on the beach, and I was camped up on the hillside above. Andreas's taverna was just a covered porch, and it had a view of the bay. The steak was goat and not bad. One time I got to meet the goat beforehand. Andreas did good business. I met the architect of the new resort and was invited to a fresh lobster dinner.

I camped all over Andreas's hillside, and Andreas wasn't happy about it. He had a small shack and wanted me to move in; he thought it would be safer. I spent a few nights in it, but I enjoyed sleeping under the stars. There was a new golf course down the road, and I had to check it out. I played only once all summer.

I would visit the beach down the trail from Vatos often. The characters camped there had a pretty sweet setup. They had a spring with fresh water. It was a good walk from Ermonos, and I always enjoyed going through Vatos. The beach was clothing-optional, and, of course, most of the time, we were nude. Almost every day a little guy with a funny hat would show up and blow his whistle. We would all head into the water, and eventually the guy would leave.

Someone once said the best parties are the ones you barely remember. I forget where this place was, but it wasn't far from Ermonos. I remember laughing, singing, and dancing with kids from all over the world. I woke up in a goat field with my arms around a lovely lady. I found love and peace in Corfu.

Greece was a military dictatorship back in 1971, and the founders of democracy lived under the rule of a junta. The people were not happy with the government, and it would take some more time for democracy to return. Today they are paying the price for being part of the European Union and still not happy. As part of a European bailout plan, Greece must radically reduce public spending and demonstrations, and strikes are a common occurrence there.

Athens is a very pretty city, and I would sleep on the roof in the Plaka District. The Acropolis and Parthenon were worth the trip.

Soon it was time to head north and home. Greece was beautiful, but soldiers and checkpoints were everywhere in Greece at the time.

Yugoslavia would be the only communist state that I would visit. It was ruled by one of Europe's longest-running dictators, Marshal Titov. I drove to Skopje and hung a left for the Adriatic. The south was very poor and had no paved roads at the time. When I passed through some towns, the kids would throw rocks at the car as I drove by.

What was good about Yugoslavia was that there was no advertising, and stores had no signs on the outside. What was bad was that I had trouble communicating, as practically no one spoke English. My German was limited to "please" and "thank you," so I did a lot of pointing and nodding.

The farther north I drove along the Adriatic coast, the prettier it got. Dubrovnik and Split were very pretty towns. It was just sad not to be able to talk with the people, as German was pretty much the only language they spoke other than their own.

I entered Switzerland through France and saw the mountain paradise for the first time. Switzerland was very clean, and the people were very proper. It had excellent food and the cheapest gasoline in Europe. I visited my old girlfriend in Geneva and found the city charming. Switzerland is divided into three areas: the French, the German, and the Italian. I liked the French part the best, but what do I know? It all was beautiful.

My first trip ended in Amsterdam. Amsterdam was one wild place back in 1971. You could sleep in Vondel Park, but I camped in the campground next to the Olympic stadium. You could take the trams anywhere, and, of course, I was a poor American tourist by that time, so I rode them for free. Back then, there were no so-called coffeehouses (pot bars) of today, but there were clubs. The Paradisio was in an old church. Back then, the hashish was stronger than pot, and you could order off a menu.

Amsterdam is my favorite city in Europe for a lot of reasons, not just because you can get high openly. The people are as friendly as Scandinavians. Back then the American Express office was a major hangout. One day I ran into a friend from Camp Roosevelt there. He told me the lottery had just happened, and the results were in the *International Herald Tribune*. I quickly got a paper and nervously scanned the dates and numbers: number 285, and no way I was going to get drafted. I screamed and yelled and jumped up and down and did a little dance. A party broke out immediately. On a trip with many happy days, it was the happiest.

I met some friends from Corfu who lived in Amsterdam. Squatting was common back then, and they had found a new building to live in. They staked the place out and were wondering if I was up for helping them. I said sure, and my job was to keep pushing the light button in the corridor while they switched out the locks. Everything went down smoothly, and they invited me to a Who concert that would be happening in a few days. I met a girl from Luxembourg, got sidetracked, and never made the show.

I took Pierre to the port of Rotterdam and shipped him back to America. I would fly back home the next day. I would visit Amsterdam more than a few times in my life. I would play golf all over the area and see many pretty places in Holland. The Dutch are unique and sophisticated. The art, canals, parks, shops, trams, food, music, and people make Amsterdam my favorite city in Europe.

After my first trip to Europe, I had my first experience with culture shock. Now that I was not in danger of being drafted, I had no reason to continue the charade of being a college student. I would work and save my money, so that I could return to Europe the next summer.

My second trip was different than my first; I no longer had a car. This trip I was the quintessential backpacker. I had a tent and a sleeping bag and mostly camped. I visited some of the same places again: London, Paris, and Amsterdam. I hitchhiked some and took a few trains, and that was how I got to Barcelona.

Spain was still ruled by Franco, who was another dictator. The people were not happy with their government. The military seemed ever present. Soldiers came on my train and found one guy who they started to beat and eventually dragged from the train.

Spain and Greece were the cheapest countries in Europe; they were also the most repressed. I took the ferry from Barcelona to Mallorca and stayed a few weeks. Ibiza was the place to go, but I was afraid of the crowds. Mallorca is pretty enough but not in Corfu's class.

I had avoided Germany on my first trip, as I'd had no desire to visit a country with that kind of history. One of my tricks to avoid hitchhiking was to ask people in campgrounds I'd stay in for a ride. If they seemed normal, I would ask where they were going and then ask for a ride. That was how I ended up in Germany.

Back then it seemed Germany was an occupied country, with American bases and troops everywhere. The people were not very friendly toward Americans, and I guess they had good reason. I was on my way to Greece to catch a boat to Israel, as my sister Sandy was still there. I arrived in Rudesheim, a fairy-tale village in the southern Rhine Valley. They were a having a wine festival, and there was good wine. I got to dance with the wine queen. The next day I got sick—really sick, so sick that I thought I was dying.

When we arrived in Munich, I needed a hospital. We spotted a line of police cars, and we must have been near the Olympic village. One of the policemen took pity on me and took me to a hospital; my ride to Greece kept going without me. I never felt more Jewish anywhere in the world as I did in Germany. When the doctor told me he was going to take some blood, I wanted my mommy. To be fair to the hospital, they took good care of me. They told me I had food poisoning, and after a few days, I was well enough to leave. The people in my ward were not happy about a sick hippie in their midst, but I got well, and the hospital never charged me a penny.

While I was sick, a group of terrorists had taken members of the Israeli Olympic team hostage. Germany doesn't have the greatest record of protecting Jewish life, and it was no surprise to me that the team wound up being butchered. I am sure if the event had happened to any other delegation, the games would have been canceled.

I left Munich by train and got to Salzburg, Austria, a very nice little city and the home of Mozart. I decided to try and hitchhike to Vienna, and I spent five hours trying to catch a ride. The rain started to come down, and it got colder, and I was mighty frustrated. That was the end of my second European trip. I caught a train to Luxembourg and flew home.

My two trips to Europe (with the exception of the ending of the second trip) were fun and positive experiences. I was now hooked on exploring and traveling the world. Seeing other cultures firsthand was a great education, and the people and friends I made along the way also provide warm memories.

Five

Enjoy Your Visit, but Please Don't Stay

After my second tour, I was still a little shook up over my hospital experience and proximity to a terror event. I was glad I didn't have to watch the terrorism on television. I was on my way to Israel, and I thought I was going to die. Traveling was fun for me, and I knew I would be on the road soon.

I went to work as a salesman for Save Mart, a chain of television and hi-fi stores all over New York City. It was fun to play with all the new toys. Videocassette recorders retailed for over two thousand dollars. The television brand of choice was Zenith, although there were less-expensive brands. I learned a bit about consumer electronics.

A Canadian friend I met in Europe invited me to his wedding in Toronto. Another childhood friend had bought some land in Oregon. I was ready for another adventure and wanted to see the West Coast. Pierre and I had traveled some miles in Europe; getting the car off the docks in Jersey was scary. Tow trucks were bringing a lot fancier cars to customs. Pierre arrived on its own power, but when I went to open the trunk, I saw the whole rear end was smashed. Evidently it was a rough crossing. Lloyds insured me, and it took a year and a half to collect the repair bills. They sent an admiral to investigate, but they had to pay, because my mom wouldn't leave them alone.

Paul, another friend from Corfu, had a wedding in Toronto which was fun. His touring sidekick Mike was the best man. I liked Toronto and still have friends who live there. Younge Street and Ontario Place were fun to visit, and the people were more laid-back than New Yorkers. In Toronto, I decided to drive across Canada and then down the coast to Oregon. I had twenty-five dollars in cash and a Gulf credit card.

Canada is a magnificent country. Once you leave a city, you really leave a city. Somewhere on Lake Superior, I met the biggest and fattest mosquitoes I ever had the pleasure of meeting. There were so many, it made it impossible to enjoy the beauty. The prairie was truly endless. My first view of the Rocky Mountains made an impression. The golden sunsets were special. I had my first experience with native Indians.

I saw a sign for a lake and decided that was where we would set up camp for the night. I had a couple of riders to share the expense of getting to Vancouver. We weren't far from Banff and Lake Louise. We found a spot on a very nice lake only a few miles from the highway. We started setting up camp, but I soon noticed a group of people standing on the ridge above camp. They were Indians, and they were just glaring at us. I decided to walk up the hill, and they started walking down the hill. They told me it wasn't safe to camp there; they said I might get "hit" if we spent the night there. I figured I could find another camping spot, so we moved on, as we had no idea whose land it was.

The Rockies were spectacular, and Vancouver was one of the prettiest cities I have ever seen. The trip across Canada was special because of the beauty of its countryside. I was glad my first crossing of the continent had been across Canada.

"The Reeg" was a childhood friend who grew up not far from my house. We had been in grade school together, and the Reeg had been at Roosevelt for a few years. After grade school, the Reeg had gone to prep school. He had dropped out of Syracuse, and I had some fun times visiting him there. My ultimate concert experience was seeing Traffic at the war memorial. *John Barleycorn Must Die* was my most-played album, and I had my first experience in a water bed somewhere on campus.

The Reeg bought twenty-five acres up Savage Creek, not far from Grants Pass, Oregon, and started a commune. Somehow, in the time it took me to cross the country, it had gone from a hippie commune to a born-again Christian commune. The place had two cabins, and both were full, so I planted my tent on the Reeg's hillside.

It seemed two of the Reeg's friends who were living in Savage Creek went on a pot run to Mexico. On their way back, they wrecked and rolled their van, and all the pot spilled out in Siskiyou County. It was probably the largest bust for the county at that time. The friends found Jesus in the county jail. When they got out, they converted the whole little community.

It was unbelievable that the Reeg was completely into praising the lord, and his lord was Jesus. I had been at the Reeg's bar mitzvah, and the Reeg had been at mine. His was different from everyone's in that he just had a party and didn't have to pray in temple. Big Ed's bar mitzvah was in Long Beach and was the best. Big Ed's dad was connected, and two rival crews got into a brawl. The police and ambulance crews had to be called. The Reeg and I witnessed it all.

I asked a couple of other people from the neighborhood where I might find some normal people. Now I had a mission to find the Mt. Mushroom natural foods restaurant. Medford, Oregon, was a town of around fifteen thousand people, it had no television station, and its largest employer was Harry & David. Southern Oregon was about to go boom. In 1973, the governor's greeting to motorists entering the state was "Enjoy your visit, but please don't stay." A popular bumper sticker was "Don't Californicate Oregon," a noble sentiment. I root for the state of Jefferson a concept of creating a state out of Southern Oregon and Northern California.

I found the Mt. Mushroom and met the owners, Skip and Sue, and the most beautiful woman in the world. Only that thunderbolt would keep me coming back to a natural foods restaurant. The only thing I could order off the menu was goat's-milk ice cream. Back then, beef wasn't natural. Anyway, we all became quick friends, as all three knew all the people up Savage Creek.

I worked for White Farms in Central Point, thanks to a recommendation from Joe's Produce in Medford. I was still living in a tent above the commune when I got everybody jobs picking corn at the farm; they quit after a day. Not long after, I got word from the commune that I was either with them or against them. I asked if I could just use the bathroom once in a while. They said no, so I needed a new home. Skip, Sue, and Bonita said I could move in with them in a house on Van Ness in Ashland.

Ashland was smaller than Medford. And it was home of the Oregon Shakespearean Festival, Southern Oregon College, and Lithia Park. The police station was next to the entrance of Lithia Park. People would get high and recreate in the park. Across the street was my favorite bar, the Log Cabin. Vito's was my favorite pizza place and second home. Ashland is one of the prettiest towns in Oregon.

Mount Ashland has a ski area, and you could go in any direction and find beauty. The Rogue River had only one dam back then, instead of the three it has today. The headwaters are still special, though, and they are not far from Crater Lake. The Rogue empties into the Pacific next to the town of Gold Beach. It is a different kind of pretty town, with better sunsets.

I liked the Illinois Valley and the Applegate country a lot. The Applegate country, of course, is much different today. It wasn't dammed back then, and we used to party up there. At one party, I met a guy from Boston and another very beautiful lady.

Alin and Sandy were friends of Bonita from Boston. She was going through a divorce, and her ex lived in Sunny Valley. (He would wind up on the big island of Hawaii.) They had a little boy who looked more like Mom than he did Dad. Alin and Sandy would move to Central Point and then on to Coos Bay. Sandy was born in Gunnison County, Colorado.

Wilton White was my boss, but he treated me like family. His kindness to me was exceptional, and I believe he genuinely liked me. I got to drive his favorite white pickup. It was a funky sixty-something Dodge with a huge doghouse attached to its rear. With that truck I delivered fresh sweet corn to Medford markets. He also made me crew boss to supervise the pear harvest. He owned a few hundred acres of pears around the valley. Wilton had three sons, and Tom, who worked on the farm, was really my boss. Another son was the Jackson County district attorney. Another was a character, I believe, who owned and operated the Junction Bar in Medford.

I would learn the beauty and bounty of agriculture from White Farms. Their farm was located on the Rogue River, underneath Table Rock. The farm had quarters for its migrant workers, and my crew was far from mellow. The pear crew was all about working fast. The more you picked, the more you earned. They were paid by the bin, and it was up to me to approve each bin. Once I rejected a bin because of punctured fruit. The worker threatened my life and went looking for a gun. I told Tom about it, and he decided to call the sheriff. The whole crew disappeared when the sheriff showed up. I never had problems after that.

The Whites would retire and sell out to Harry & David. Last time I went through, Tom's house in Jacksonville was for sale. Central Point and the Rogue Valley had boomed and Californicated since 1973 and '74. I sure miss the old places.

Eventually the harvest ended, and I needed a new job. Oregon was mighty depressed back then, and still is in some places today. I had some friends who were tree planters, and that sounded like fun, so I thought I would give it a try.

Around that time, I killed Pierre. I didn't mean to, but it happened. The week before, I brought the car to a shop located in the town of Rogue River for normal service. This guy supposedly specialized in foreign cars but screwed the timing up, and eventually I got the car overheated. Like the idiot that I can sometimes be, I poured cold water over a hot engine block and cracked it. I had to sell Pierre for parts to the idiot who had wrecked the timing.

Tree planting was a difficult job for me, and I lasted only two days. The terrain was anything but smooth and flat, and, of course, you had to be fast. It would have been fine if I could plant at my own pace, but you had to keep up with the group. I could not keep up and was usually separated from the group.

It was time to start thinking of wintering in Israel. I could not find work. The most beautiful woman in the world would always be a nice dream, but we were not going to be a couple. The Reeg and his friends were still praising the lord. It was time to move on.

On my last night in Ashland, an ominous omen appeared in the night sky. A wildfire broke out on the ridge above town. The sky was orange, and if the wind blew the wrong way, the town could have burned. It didn't, but it was a scary sight.

When you look at that ridge today, you would never know that a wildfire had happened there.

The Reeg married Roxy, and they, of course, lived happily ever after. They had three sons and are living in the LA area. The Reeg distributes light bulbs for Westinghouse and is a grandpa. I ran into him in Israel after the intifada ended. He was wearing a Star of David and was traveling the holy land with his church group. I asked him what he thought of the place, and he spouted some tourist propaganda, saying he loved the place and would come back. The Reeg had no clue about Israel, but I wish him well.

Six

October 6, 1973

The flight to Israel from Oregon is long, and I had to change planes in New York. I didn't call home when I was in New York, and I felt guilty about it. When I got to Israel, I headed for Netanya and settled on the beach. That night I was robbed of my wallet while I was asleep. I had put my passport and traveler's checks in my sleeping bag but left the wallet in my pants. The police later found my wallet minus the cash. In all my travels, it was the only time I was ever robbed.

I decided to learn Hebrew and heard of a program managed by one of the kibbutz movements. My sister Sandy now spoke Hebrew, and I didn't like the fact that she could communicate with my brother-in-law Nachum, while I had no idea what she was saying. My grandma spoke Yiddish with my mom, but I could usually figure out what they were saying. Anyway, I found the kibbutz movement (Ichud Habonim) and asked to be signed up for the program. They asked me where in the country I wanted to live, and I requested the Sachne area. I was told to report to Hamadia on October 8, pending the passing of my physical. The program involved was studying half a day and working half a day, and it would last six months.

I looked up a friend of Sandy and Nachum's who lived in Ramle, a small town between Tel Aviv and Jerusalem. He had visited America and served with my brother-in-law in the air force. He invited me to stay with him and his father, so I headed to Ramle. Baruch has a twin brother, Yacov, who was still in the air force back then. Yacov was married, and his wife's dad was a partner in an old-age home. I got to hang out there a bit and met some very nice people.

The night of October 5 started the holiday of Yom Kippur, and we had a feeling something might be wrong when one of the cousins stationed up in the Golan was denied leave, due to a Syrian buildup of forces on the other side of the border. Yom Kippur is the holiest and most sacred holiday in the Jewish religion. In Israel, everything shuts down: there are no cars on the road and no radio or television. Back then, television was new there, and most people still had no television at home.

We went to synagogue that morning, and the feeling that something was wrong persisted. We spotted cars and military trucks on the highway. At temple, men were being picked out of services and told to report to their bases. At noon the radio came on and started calling reserve units. Yacov was called and told to report back to base. Baruch and I drove him to his base near Rehovot, and they both felt war was approaching. Sure enough, at two that afternoon, the air-raid sirens blared, and the war started.

The Egyptian army crossed the canal and Syria invaded the Golan in north. I was not a happy camper; I was supposed to be in Hamadia in a couple of days, and Hamadia was only twenty-five miles from the battle in the Golan. I had no desire to be in a war, but a war was happening. A countrywide blackout was put into effect, and car headlights were painted over.

Real news was hard to come by, and the next day, my friend asked his friend, the chief of police, to come and talk with me. He told me it was not safe to go to Hamadia. I listened and thought maybe he was right. I decided to call my mom back home, which was a big mistake. Mom didn't care about the war; she wanted to know what happened to Pierre. For the next ten minutes, my mom yelled at me about the death of Pierre. I decided to go to Hamadia; it would be easier to face the Arabs than to face my mom. A lot of countries were trying to get their citizens out of Israel. I could have easily left the country but was too scared to deal with my mom.

The Yom Kippur War snapped Israel out of its feeling of invincibility. This war lasted a lot longer than six days. The price for American support of the war was no preemptive attack on the troops massed along its borders. Nixon would send all the weapons they needed, but Israel had to absorb the first blow. In Israel, every single life has meaning and importance, and that is why they will trade a thousand prisoners for one soldier. Over three thousand Israeli lives were lost in the Yom Kippur War. America did not save Israel during the war; Israel saved itself. Yes, America did ship weapons during the war, but those weapons had no bearing on the fight.

Can you imagine giving your life up for six months to fight a war? That was what most Israeli men had to do. All men eighteen years of age in Israel are compelled to do three years of mandatory service. After that, men are assigned to reserve units and usually spend three weeks training each year. During the Yom Kippur War, however, the war-reserve units stayed in service six months. Their jobs, their wives, their kids, and their lives were put on hold.

The first few days of the war were a disaster for Israel. It took that long to get the reserves organized. The reserves saved Israel.

The shock and trauma of this war's impact on Israeli society cannot be overstated. After this war, many Israelis immigrated elsewhere. The political fallout would drive the socialists from power. The war's economic impact would be devastating. After the war, Israel experienced hyperinflation and the destruction of its currency. Indeed, the Arab oil embargo not only brought gas lines to America, it ended the days of cheap gasoline. I was paying around a quarter a gallon when I left, and when I returned I was paying around a dollar for the same gallon.

Sometimes I wondered if I would see 1974. Israel had nuclear weapons back then, and after the first few days of the war, I thought those bombs might be used. America's going on nuclear alert helped end the major fighting. The two bloodiest battles of the war took place at Chinese Farm in Sinai and the Vale of Tears in the Golan.

When I got to Hamadia on the eighth, it was surrounded by troops and their weapons, and I felt safe. Jordan had massed troops along its border but did not attack. Eventually some of the troops around Hamadia would go to Africa.

At night the sky would light up from the distant fire in the Golan in the north. One of my first jobs was pulling irrigation pipes out of a freshly planted minefield. One day an F4 phantom jet moving fast at treetop level from Jordan buzzed me. The two puffs of white smoke that appeared in the sky after the jet passed meant it was being shot at.

After the jet incident, a lot of my fellow students decided to leave. My class had started with thirty students and finished with eight, including myself. Every evening we would go to the bomb shelter under the dining room to watch the news on television. We never learned much, but watching the news brought everyone together. We did get the *Jerusalem Post*, the only daily English paper in the country at the time. Wolf Blitzer of CNN fame was a writer for the *Jerusalem Post* back then, and the only good thing in the paper was Shuldig's comic strip, *Dry Bones*. We didn't learn much from the paper either.

The saddest night of the war was when we learned one of Hamadia's sons had been killed. He was killed when Egyptian soldiers overran his bunker on the Bar Lev line on the first day of the war. His parents did not receive formal notification for almost three weeks. That night at dinner, no one talked, and not a sound was heard.

The main lesson I took from the war was that it took sacrifice to have a country. The kids in Hamadia would spend their nights in bomb shelters during the war, and so would a few volunteers. When I got to Hamadia, I was assigned a bed in the student house, and it had a shower and a bathroom. I didn't like a lot of the students, so I was allowed to move in with the volunteers. I was stepping down as far as services in the house were concerned but got to hang around with much nicer people. I was more a volunteer than a student anyway. With most of the men gone, they needed workers more than they did students. I worked more than I studied and learned my Hebrew from the people who lived there. We were paid ten dollars a month and got thirty cigarette coupons.

I was no longer a tourist in Israel; I had become a temporary resident. I felt extremely productive and appreciated by the members of Hamadia. I was assigned a family whom I could sit with for the Friday-night meal. It would take a few months before I would meet my adoptive dad, as he was fighting in Africa. I felt a part of many homes in Hamadia. I will always consider it my home in Israel. When I am not in Hamadia, not a day goes by when I don't think of its beauty and its warm and generous people. Hamadia is why I love Israel.

Seven

Hamadia

Hamadia was founded in the forties by a hearty group of pioneers. It is named after a former ruler of Turkey, Hamid. The early days, of course, were no paradise. Malaria was a constant threat, and the early settlers lived in tents. They fought Arabs with sticks back then.

Hamadia was a border kibbutz, and groups of soldiers would stay there as part of their army service. Some parts of each group (Nahal) would wind up settling in the kibbutz, and so the population grew. In 1973, kibbutzniks considered themselves the elite of society. Israel was a socialist country, and the government subsidized agriculture. Hamadia was a rich kibbutz, and it had over five thousand acres of ground that were farmed. It had a successful door factory as well as a fiberglass fabrication plant that specialized in playground equipment.

The food was excellent and of high quality. Back then, nobody paid for food, housing, utilities, or taxes. No one owned cars, but the kibbutz did, and all you had to do was sign up on a sheet, and you could use one. The gasoline was on the kibbutz as long as you stayed in the area. Each member got two weeks of vacation a year and could stay in the movement's resorts for free. If you wanted a college education, all you had to do was sign up, and the kibbutz would pay for a certain number of students each year to attend college.

Each member received the same compensation, whether he or she ran the factory or just emptied the trash. Each member had to take a turn in the kitchen, and men were required to stand guard at night. Back then, annual compensation for members was almost five hundred dollars. The kibbutz had a clinic where visiting doctors would come. It also had a fire truck, and you better have had a good excuse if you weren't going out on a fire call.

In 1973, kibbutzniks were snobs, because they lived better than did most of the population. They made less money, for sure, but they had no overhead. Almost forty years later, the roles have mostly reversed. Hamadia went bankrupt, and the population is less than half of what it was and is mostly retired.

With most of the men gone on reserve duty, there was no shortage of work. The people in Hamadia raised cattle, fish, and chickens and grew wheat, cotton, potatoes, onions, sugar beets, peanuts, melons, carrots, corn, and alfalfa hay. There were also pomegranates, oranges, grapefruits, olives, and dates. There was, at the time, a very sophisticated irrigation system. I worked where I was wanted.

In the winter months after a storm, we would fish where the rivers met the Mediterranean Sea. Fishing on the Yarkon was an all-night affair. We would run along the waters with a small net and scoop little baby fish out of the breaking surf. The little silver fish are called *burim* and, with time, would grow quite large in the ponds. If we started getting tired, the boss would produce a bottle of Sheva, Sheva, Sheva (777), the worst brandy in the world. I think that brandy could have powered a tractor. After dawn, we would go to the pancake house for breakfast.

Sending chickens and fish to market was a dirty, tedious job. The worst job, aside from picking pomegranates, was cleaning the chicken houses and shoveling chicken shit. We would feed the chicken shit to the fish—nothing went to waste.

Working in the olive trees was laid-back, and so was moving wheat from the field to the storage bins. Working irrigation was always fun, but maintaining the pipes was tedious. My favorite assignment was working for Mordi. Mordi was a civil engineer who needed an assistant on a regular basis.

Mordi and Orly are amazing people, and both lived through hell. Mordi was from Dresden, Germany, and walked to Israel after Hitler came to power. His wife Orly was from Czechoslovakia and survived Dachau and other Nazi death camps. They were very nice to me and always fed me chocolate.

Mordi had engineered many of the Bet Shean Valley fishponds. Today half the fish sold in Israel comes from the Bet Shean Valley. We were involved in a pipeline project that would pump water from the Jordan River. We laid out a new irrigation system on Hamadia hill. We also did work on a new reservoir and a memorial.

One day I almost killed Mordi by accident. We were working on the pipeline project, and I was on top of a hill, and Mordi was below me when I leaned against an iron post, and it gave way. The post landed on top of Mordi's head. He is a tough man in a country of tough men. Mordi and Orly are both in their nineties today and too tough to die.

Mordi got me to do things I never thought possible. I would walk through a field of thorns only for Mordi. Mordi would bring me a special breakfast featuring chocolate spread. He was the best boss in Hamadia.

Sometimes I would sing James Taylor's "Walkin' on a Country Road" to the Jordanian troops who were watching us work. The *zor* (Hebrew for "neighborhood"), which was the area next to the river, was the prettiest place to work in Hamadia. I was lucky enough to work there quite a bit. I worked cotton down there, as well as fish. The zor had hundreds of acres of fishponds, and Jews from Melbourne, Australia, built a reservoir.

Leon was a volunteer from Melbourne and had been through the *ulpan* before me. Leon and I got promoted, and we had much classier digs. We now had a toilet, a shower, and a small kitchen. Leon was looking for love and finally found it, and is a happy man to this day. Leon, Aubrey, Bernie, and the ever-alluring Margot made up the Australian all-stars in Hamadia. Leon and I were now guests, as opposed to volunteers, which meant we now had the same responsibility as a member. I made a deal with the work manager, and we never had to wash dishes, but we did have to do guard duty. We qualified with a M14 and learned how to clean our rifles together. Guard duty wasn't bad if you could talk a lady into hanging out with you in the tower.

I would meet many wonderful ladies during my time living in Hamadia. The best were the Israeli soldiers sent to work there as part of their army service. Orna denies it today, but Yoav will verify that the sight of bikini-clad soldiers marching to the swimming pool is not bad. The most fun job I had was spraying weeds in newly planted cotton with female soldiers. I had a Massey Ferguson 180 outfitted with four chairs and four sprayers on the front. Orna was a main target for me. She was a sergeant and answered only to the lieutenant, but there were at least ten soldiers under them. Whenever Sarge was in the chair, we would take long breaks at a spring called En Soda (*en* is Hebrew for "not"). Orna wasn't interested in me but did marry a close friend in Bucky. Bucky, Yoav, Gera, and Yael were all born in Hamadia. Their mom was a teacher, and their dad ran the Israeli domestic airline Arkia. Yoav and Bucky were warriors, and they both would meet the most beautiful woman in the world.

After the war ended, I needed a break, as there suddenly was a whole bunch of strangers back from the war. I went back to Oregon and got a place in Ashland. I would go back to Hamadia after a few months away. Some new friends would visit me in Ashland, in southern Oregon country. When Bucky and Gadi showed up in Ashland, everyone treated them well, and they even gave an interview on the Ashland country-music station.

Hamadia had a disco, and it would have a couple of locations. I remember some steamy dances. Today Hamadia has a small pub, and sometimes it is host to many popular artists. I guess people are still dancing there.

The most beautiful woman in the world would show up in Hamadia right after I had to leave. It seemed that she had a crush on Bucky. Orna or Bonita? Bucky did well, and I believe he is a happier man today. I always had a crush on his sister but never got anywhere with her. She too is happily married. Leon had more luck with her than I did but it never got serious.

Bucky's family is another family I will always cherish. His dad was one of the few people in Hamadia with a private phone, and he was always good for a ride to Tel Aviv (you had to be on time, because he would not wait a single minute beyond the appointed time). Bucky's mom is a pretty smart cookie and usually gave me a hard time.

I used to hike a lot on my days off. I would hike to Gesher, Neve Etan, and Maoz Haim and play tennis. I would hike to Bet Shean and, of course, to Sachne. I would sneak in from Nir David. I walked from Tiberias to Semach. I walked to the spring, I walked along the Jordan River, and I walked the Hamadia Hills. I never played golf there at the time, but I sure walked a lot.

Arieh, in charge of most of the field crops, was a tough boss. He was tough to please. The most stress for me was when I had to prepare an open field for the planting of sugar beets. Yigal was the boss; he was demoted to sugar beets. Yigal ran the kibbutz during the war and is a nice guy. Arieh would be the true judge. I made rows that were five hundred meters long, and they had to be straight. I thought there might be a few bows in my work, but Arieh said I did a good job, and I knew I could farm if I had to. Arieh and his family also remain very special to me. His intellectual wife is like another sister to me.

I played basketball in Hamadia. Back then, Israel had multiple professional leagues, and Hamadia was in the worst league. We were pretty awful, but we had fun. We sure ran a lot. Once the fighting ended, it got easier for social events. I was an extra egg in a Purim skit. I took a bunch of high-schoolers to Yad Eliyahu (Tel Aviv's Madison Square Garden) to watch Macabi basketball. I don't think Macabi could score fifty against Van Buren. It was a fun time.

The Black War had an effect on everyone in Israel, and everyone was hurting—some hurt more than others. My adoptive dad had a party, and I was invited. The reserves had been released back into society. Men I barely knew were back from service. A couple of dozen people sung songs for four hours. No one spoke, but everyone had a song, and it seemed all the songs were sad. It was an emotional deal. It would take time.

Of my class that finished, Hiya would marry in Hamadia but eventually move back to Toronto. Diane would have to be evacuated out of Beirut. Janice would move back to Jersey. Chuck and Sue stayed in Neve Etan. Lisa went on to the Technion, found herself a husband, and was in Philadelphia the last I heard. Not much of a graduating class.

Tony and Mike were my old volunteer roomies from England. Mike once visited me in Colorado, where he met a lady and got married before going back to Knutsford, but not before almost destroying my snowmobile. He started it, and it took off without him. The snowmobile flew off the top of the mesa and wound up in Ohio Creek. I spoke to Tony once after the war and he seemed mad at the world.

Harry was from Philadelphia and was destined for Hollywood. Harry was the source of much laughter and trouble. He somehow became an extra on a Burt Lancaster film shooting near Eilat. A few volunteers from Hamadia were extras in the movie *Moses the Lawgiver*. Harry had a scene where he got stoned with rocks thrown by the locals. He is now a representative for Consumer Electronic Products in the Hollywood area. Mandy Patinkin worked one day in Hamadia. He was a better actor than he was a farmer.

During my time in Israel, there were volunteers from Sweden, Holland, Switzerland, France, South Africa, Canada, and Detroit. None stayed permanently. Only Mike from Nova Scotia, who was in the Ulpan after I was, would stay and find a love and raise his daughters in Hamadia. I seriously thought of staying. Staying would have meant going into the army.

Quite out of the blue, my decision was made for me. One morning I got a telegram from Sandy that My mom was sick and was going into the hospital for surgery. Sandy thought it was time to come home. I needed to be with my mom and be supportive through her illness.

The dream of the founding fathers of Hamadia would die. Socialism was no match for capitalism. What Hamadia was once it will never be again: the sacrifice and hard work of a community of equals. What a noble concept, but this self-sufficient world was corrupted by greed.

Hamadia has an elevation well below sea level. The beauty of the land remains. A national park was built around En Soda. The beauty and education about life I found there were better than college for me. As Garth Brooks sang, "I've got friends in low places."

Eight
US Electric

The trip back to New York was hard; my mom was sick and facing surgery. I don't remember the name of the hospital, but I do remember the name of my mom's doctor. The doctor had worked on Happy Rockefeller, so I knew Mom had found the best. He gave her ten more good years of life.

My family was not happy with me. My oldest sister, Esta, blamed my mom's illness on me. The stress of my lifestyle had caused it, according to her. By now my two brothers-in-law were in the old family business. My oldest brother-in-law Sam worked for my dad. When my dad died, his best salesmen took most of the business and started their own. Sam was left with almost nothing. My mom helped keep the business going, until eventually he found a line he could make money with. Once he did, he changed the name of the business. When my Israeli brother-in-law got to New York, he needed a job, so he went to work for my older brother-in-law. There was no room in the business for me.

My older brother-in-law did tell me to visit one of his customers. I did and was offered a position at the bottom of the totem pole at US Electrical Supply Company. Everybody who worked there was a character. Allie Kahn (former president of the North Shore Democratic Club) was the infamous counterman. Andy, Leo, Lester, and Joe kept the product moving. The owners worked the business too and were family. I fit right in.

I got my first and only apartment in the North Shore Towers on the edge of Queens and Nassau County. They were three brand-new high rises located just off the Grand Central Parkway. Back then the place was new and mostly empty, and the rent was cheaper than living in the city. It was pretty fancy living for me. The complex had a shopping mall and indoor and outdoor pools. The old Glen Oaks golf course was on the property. The Chase Manhattan Bank would eventually convert the Towers to condos. The place had a great restaurant that was owned by the same guy who ran Andre's, a Great Neck institution. It also had a good bakery and deli. The health club was new and clean, and life was certainly different from Oregon and Hamadia.

One day I decided to play basketball back in the old neighborhood at PS 205. I got into a game, and, of course, I knew most of the players. My childhood buddy Malkin decided to come down on my ankle. I was in agony, and my foot was twitching in shock. My friends decided to carry me off the court and then, as there was a ready replacement available, return to the game. I had to crawl to my car and drive to the emergency room at Long Island Jewish Hospital. They took X-rays, and the diagnosis was a high ankle sprain. They taped me up and gave me crutches. I was on crutches for the next two weeks. My friends felt guilty, or maybe they just wanted to see how much pain I was in. They all showed up at my apartment that evening. My new apartment had its first party, and my pain lessened for a little while.

US Electric was a wholesale distributor and sold mostly to independent hardware stores. The warehouse ran from Warren to Murray Street, a couple of blocks from the World Trade Center and City Hall. US Electric sold many products: wiring devices manufactured by Eagle and Leviton; wire and cable, fuses, FuseStats, and Fusetrons; Progress lighting fixtures; Farberware pots and pans; General Electric light bulbs and small appliances and radios; Timex watches, fans, and space heaters; Mr. Coffee and Bunn coffeemakers; and Hobart heavy-duty mixers. My company catalog was thicker than the Manhattan phone book.

I learned to pick, pack, and ship orders and then got to work for Leo down in the dungeon, which was the light-bulb department. When Allie went to lunch or needed a break, I would be called up to work the counter. US Electric was wholesale only, and it did have a walk-in trade. My goal was to be in outside sales. Eventually a salesman, Abe, did retire, and I was assigned his accounts and routes.

Abe was a gentle soul and a good salesman. He helped my transition and had solid accounts. They were located in

Jersey, Brooklyn, Queens, Nassau, and Suffolk Counties. Eventually I expanded his account base and felt I did a good job.

One of Abe's accounts was located in the Greenpoint section of Brooklyn. The whole store was behind bulletproof glass. The owner was not a great payer, but after he did pay me, he always escorted me to my car while packing a pistol.

Donna Electric was not one of Abe's old accounts but was a dormant house account. It was in the fifties on the east side of Manhattan. Donna was the daughter of the owner and a lady I could fall in love with. It never happened, but US Electric got a lot more business out of Donna Electric.

I had a couple of accounts all the way out on Long Island, near the Hamptons. I would visit my grandma's brother every so often. Grandma had died, but her youngest brother was still kicking. He had an estate on Heather Lane, a short distance to the Atlantic Ocean in the town of East Hampton. I would take some presents and buy him lunch. Uncle Manny had never married, and some of his famous exes included Lucille Ball and Dina Merrill. One day at lunch he asked me if I wanted to learn his best pickup line, and, of course, I said I did. So he called over a cute waitress and said, "Baby doll, do you want to come home with me? I've got a lot of money."

Uncle Manny was well into his eighties, and I don't think that was a great line, but who knows? It didn't work on that waitress that day.

Uncle Manny did have a lot of money, and he had over three hundred nieces and nephews. Every time any family visited, he would promise to leave you a million dollars in his will.

When he did die years later, the executor of the estate sent me a copy of his will. He wanted me to sign off that the will was OK by me. I know a lot of family never got a copy of his will. My oldest sister would not sign off; she got nothing and wasn't happy. I got nothing and signed off, because I expected nothing. Uncle Manny was a Jewish pioneer in East Hampton and helped build the Jewish Center of the Hamptons. A lot of his estate went to the state of New York. A cousin who was a Hollywood screenwriter became a buddy of Uncle Manny at the end of his life, and he got a good chunk of money. An ex-girlfriend got a little money, and so did a poor cousin. All the rest of the family got nothing, including those uncles and cousins each promised a million.

* * *

In the summer of 1976, some friends of mine from Oregon decided to move to Colorado and get married. I was invited to the wedding, so I headed west to check it out. Colorado was just as pretty as Oregon but seemed more affluent. It was in the process of an economic boom.

The bride, Sandy, was a local who grew up at Jack's Cabin, about halfway between Gunnison and Crested Butte. Alin, the groom, was from Boston, and his dad came out for the event. The most beautiful woman in the world did not attend, but her ex-husband did. That was it for foreigners, as the rest of the guests were family and friends of Sandy.

The wedding took place at Irwin Lodge, above Lake Irwin and near the top of Kebler Pass. The place was as pretty as anywhere on the planet. Alin, his dad, and I headed out of the town of Gunnison, and everything was fine until we hit Lake Irwin. We could see the lodge when Alin said, "I'm not sure I know how to get there." His father shut up, and I kept my mouth closed but thought, Uh-oh. We had been on dirt roads for miles, but now the road narrowed, and we went through one fork after another. After about the sixth fork, Alin stopped the truck, got out, and announced that he had no idea how to get to his own wedding. Alin's dad let out some bad words and then shut up. I said that maybe someone who knew how to get there would come by.

We would wait about two hours, and eventually a friend of the family would find us. Now the fun could begin, right? Wrong. When we finally entered the lodge, the moaning and groaning was audible. The looks on the guests' faces were not exactly warm and friendly. When the reverend pronounced the couple man and wife, no one uttered a sound. I wanted to clap and shout "mazel tov" but was afraid I would be taken out back and shot. Eventually the couple made their way to the bar to receive congratulations. This was the first wedding I had been to where you had to buy your own drinks. I met Sandy's dad for the first time, and he mostly growled at me.

Aside from attending the strangest wedding I had ever seen, I got to see some of the Gunnison country. I got to see the Ohio Creek Valley for the first time and crossed Ohio Pass. I traveled over Kebler and McClure Passes and met some real characters. A seed was planted, and it would take some more time, but I would return.

I wanted to be in New York mostly for my mom's sake. I felt guilty about her sickness and tried to behave myself. After a couple of years, I knew I didn't want to live in New York City or its suburbs. My mom was healthy again and now had five grandsons to fuss over. My sisters were in their own bubble and not a lot of fun to be around. Sandy had never liked her older sister, Esta, but now they were in business together.

The sudden friendship between my sisters would not last. The business would fold, and my sisters would not talk to each other for many years. I knew lots of people in New York and knew the game that had to be played in order to survive there. I felt more alone in the city than in any wilderness. My family had no interest in ever living anywhere but the city. My mom felt civilization ended at the borders of New York City. It was time to move on.

US Electric was a great company to work for. I learned much about business there. I wish it were still in existence today. Selling is not an easy art, and I was always treated with patience and kindness.

I still thought about Hamadia every day and missed the place. I knew that if I went back, I would have to do military service for at least a year and a half. I could have any education or vocation I wanted on the kibbutz, but I had to serve first. I just did not feel up to the sacrifice it would have taken.

I played quite a bit of golf in New York during my time there. I mostly played at Bethpage, and sometimes I would play with my oldest nephew. My nephews were starting to grow up, and I would miss them the most. They were basically good kids and always fun to play with. When Alin wrote and said he was starting a new business in the town of Gunnison, it was time to go. I just didn't want to play the game in New York anymore.

Nine

The Community That Won't Admit It Exists

This is the view of Mount Carbon from Whistling Streams.

When I got to Gunnison country in early 1978, it was a different place than what it is today. The town of Gunnison is a lot more progressive than it used to be. The college is still in business, although now they call it a university. The town now has six stoplights, and back then it had two. An ice arena, softball fields, a community center with an indoor pool, a whitewater park, a sky observatory, a new jail, and new schools had not yet been established when I showed up.

The Cattleman's Days Rodeo still happens every July and is one of the oldest rodeo events in America. The mining companies of AMAX and Homestake made a lot of noise back then but are gone today. Gunnison residents have a lot to be proud of today.

The town of Crested Butte, which is twenty-five miles down the road, was also much different than it is today. The ski area has grown some and has a new owner. The streets are now paved, and there is a new high school. The Grubstake is gone, but the Nickel is still in business. The infamous Sunshine Bath House is long gone. The Soupcon and Le Bosque, two world-class restaurants, are still in business. Crested Butte is much more sedate than the wild, anything-goes town it used to be. What makes Gunnison and Crested Butte so special is the unchanged, beautiful countryside that surrounds the area.

My old buddy Alin had started a hi-fi shop on Main Street in Gunnison, and when I showed up, he took me on as a partner. Sandy's dad was a partner in the family ranch with his brother Tim, and I would work for Dave, Sandy's dad, mostly at Jack's Cabin. The ranch was over five thousand acres, and I would mostly feed cows in the morning. I would fight Dave for the pitchfork, because feeding was warmer than driving the horse sleigh. Back then Gunnison had extremely cold winters, and it was not uncommon to go six weeks and not see the temperature rise above zero degrees Fahrenheit. Of course it would warm up to snow.

My first experience in a whiteout happened on my way up to Jack's Cabin to help Dave feed. I wasn't far from the ranch when I lost all visibility on the road. Everything was solid white, and I had no idea what to do, so I just turned on my flashers and stopped. Well, after a few minutes, a state trooper pulled in behind me, got out of the car, and asked me what I was doing. When I told him, he asked me why I hadn't pulled off the road, I told him that I thought I had, because I couldn't see where the road was. Well, I am sure the trooper could tell I was scared, and he seemed like a nice guy. He gave me a look that asked, "Are you for real?" and then said to follow him. I could barely make out his flashing lights, but I had a police escort to work that morning.

I would also hay in the summer, and the ranch had a unique system of haying, which involved stacking the hay loose. We would drive "doodlebugs" to push the hay to the stacker. Lunch for the hay crew would be the best part of the day and was like a great feast.

In the afternoons I would work at the shop in Gunnison. Back then we were a struggling new business, and most of our early customers were college kids. We were located in the old theater building, and we shared the building with a kids-clothing store called the Peanut Gallery and a T-shirt shop run by the bombastic Cheryl. In the old projection room, Rita cut hair. We all got along, although the owners of the Peanut Gallery would complain when I demonstrated the speakers with Earth, Wind, & Fire.

* * *

Bolinas is a beautiful small town north of San Francisco. My cousin Curt has lived there for a long time. Just north of Stinson Beach, there is no road sign to point the way to Bolinas. The state of California has tried to put up a road sign on Highway 1, but every time they have, some townspeople would make sure it disappeared. Now Bolinas is a classy place, and it has a post office and a school. It has a volunteer fire department, and, best of all, it is located next to the Pacific Ocean. People who live there admit they live in

Bolinas, even though they have no road sign pointing the way to get there.

I mention Bolinas because you might have thought it was the community I was referring to in this chapter. It is not.

I was living in the Mansion, which was a couple of boxcars converted into a residence. I was living with Sandy's stepbrother, Mr. B, and he was building a log house right next door. As soon as it was habitable, I would move in, but Mr. B would wait until the plumbing worked. Thirty-five years later, the house isn't quite finished. I was looking to buy land and build a house. I had a little money from my dad, and I was looking hard. Almost every place I looked at would have been a better decision than the one I made, but hindsight is twenty-twenty.

Fondando was a friend who was also a realtor, and one day he took me up the Ohio Creek Valley and showed me some amazing land. He said the only drawback was that it was part of a subdivision; I thought it was no big deal. I was a naive idiot. The land was beautiful, and Ohio and Pass Creeks bordered the property. It had a mesa in between, where I would build my house. The views were 360 degrees and very special. Carbon Peak rose to an elevation of over twelve thousand feet and was one view. The Anthracite Range with Ohio Peak was another. The Castles and the West Elk Wilderness Area were another. You could see back down the valley, all the way to Sawtooth Dome and the Continental Divide seventy-five miles away. I would eventually buy seven lots, totaling over forty acres.

The subdivision has eighty-two lots behind a locked gate and another twenty or so across the road. It had originally been part of a ranch owned by an ex-governor of Colorado. The lower part of the ranch is close to Gunnison and had more lots and more development. Whistling Streams (not its real name) had only twelve houses at the time and no year-round residents when I started to build on the property.

Whistling Streams is the community that won't admit it exists. Most of its property owners live elsewhere and, because the place is so beautiful, don't care about a community. They can't be bothered with the details of a community, because they are lucky if they get to spend two weeks a year there. So the homeowners' association let people who don't live there have exclusive access while the property owners pay all the expenses. Of course it is still that way today. The association leases the open-space land to a cattle operation, and, of course, the property owners pay for that privilege in the form of dues to the association. No property owners receive compensation for the cattle lease, and previously the lawsuit funds were used however the homeowners' association saw fit. The funds from the lease of my land wound up in the association's general fund. Of course the cattle operation doesn't maintain the land and abuses certain areas, because no one cares. Because the lower subdivisions are mostly year-round residents, they control the homeowners' association. The homeowners' association is comprised of five different subdivisions, each with their own very different covenants. The people of Whistling Streams just want to be left alone and don't care.

That first summer, I got the electric company to run electric lines to my home site. Back then, the electric company was happy to have a new customer, and they hooked up a temporary outlet at no charge. The developers had agreed to a bond that would be paid back over twenty years to run electricity to each individual lot at no charge. Of course the electric company never fully complied with the agreement.

Yes, they installed electricity at no charge to lot owners who requested it, but, when the bond was paid off, they charged individual lot owners thousands for the privilege.

I also dug a well that first summer. I hired a crusty gentleman from Oklahoma, who charged me twenty dollars a foot. I showed up on the second day of drilling and found the driller in a funk. When I asked what was wrong, the driller answered that he had hit water at fifty feet. I was delighted and relieved, as drilling for water and finding it was no certainty. My well had a flow rate of ten gallons a minute, but even better, the water tested pure and tasted great. The well driller talked me into drilling another fifty feet for a reservoir. The driller was disappointed that the well would not be deeper. He was also disappointed that he had not found natural gas, as he said the mesa was the perfect geological formation to find it. When it came time to legalize my well with the state of Colorado, I named it the Hamadia well. I was lucky; few homeowners have good wells in Whistling Streams, and I never had a water problem.

I built my house the following summer. During the winter, I found and bought an energy-efficient home-design book. I found a design I liked and sent away for plans. I received three eight-and-a-half-by-eleven sheets showing the different elevations. Mr. B and a neighbor, Bedge, and I built the house. It would be slightly less than fifteen hundred square feet and energy-efficient.

Back then the county building inspector was Mr. B's old shop teacher from high school. He was a nice guy. When we went to him with our three pieces of paper, he wasn't happy. Mr. B assured the inspector that he would be building the house, and so, reluctantly, the inspector charged me forty-five dollars and issued my building permit. Today it costs thousands more and requires an engineer's review to get a building permit.

We had a problem when we first started to build. I was supposed to have a party the day before construction would start. The problem was that it stormed that day, and no one showed up to party. The next day we had a full keg of Heineken on the jobsite. We would work a few hours and then start drinking. A job that should have taken us two weeks (building the cinder-block foundation) took us six weeks.

Back then Whistling Streams had four year-round residents who lived off the county road. No one lived year-round behind the gate. I was the first, and today there are around twelve year-round residents. Back then the road was not plowed beyond the gate, and my house was at least half a mile from the county road. We luckily closed in the house before the road became impassable. That was a snowy year, and we lost the road Thanksgiving Day.

I had spent a hundred dollars on a well-used, lightweight snowmobile from Irwin Lodge. We tried to keep working on the inside, but it kept snowing, and by the time Mr. B and Bedge would arrive from town, they would start worrying about the road and then leave. I decided to shut it down and wait until the snow was gone, which was on June 1 that year.

I had met my future ex-wife, and her dad had a cabin off the county road across the creek from my old house. I would spend my first winter in Whistling Streams there. We had friends in Lake City, and one was a master rock layer. My old house had a cinder-block chimney, and earlier that summer I had picked enough moss rock to cover it. My future wife and I were going to Australia and New Zealand for a vacation. My friend agreed to move into our place while we were gone to do the rockwork. He would have to dig the rock out from under six feet of snow. He hauled in the cement on my snowmobile and sled. He melted snow for water to mix the cement.

The trip to Australia and New Zealand was a lot of fun. We met Bucky and Orna, who were on their honeymoon in Sydney and would travel down to Melbourne to visit Leon and Aubrey. One of the highlights of our trip was our time in Noosa. Some locals told us about a great beach. It was a long hike in, but, when we got there, the beach was beautiful. The people there were completely naked, and there was a cricket match going on. Nude cricket, I am sure, is played only in Australia. We would meet up with Bucky and Orna again in New Zealand on the south island in the town of Queenstown. We had fun traveling together. Back then the people we met actually liked Americans, which was not the case on my travels in Europe. When we were lost, which was often, people would go out of their way to put us on the right road. I hope that I will visit again.

When we got home, the chimney work was done. My house felt like a home, and I moved in. My future wife waited until the plumbing worked. The house was finally done, and it had taken almost a year (we started in August and finished in July). I now had my own energy-efficient house with a very special view. It was time to build the fence, and I had no clue I was about to enter a four-year nightmare.

When the developer sold me the property, he told me that I owned it, and that I could build or create anything I wanted, as long as I didn't violate county guidelines. I thought about building a pond and maybe a few golf holes. The developer ran the Architectural Control Committee, and they approved my fence. At that time, the homeowners' association leased the subdivision out to a ranching operation. The ranching operation abused the lease, and they ran about eight hundred pair in the subdivision. A pair is a mom and her calf. They never maintained the ditches, as required by lease, and didn't care about the owners of property within their lease. My land was in the first pasture, which was the largest and had the best grazing. There were four different pastures in total, but the cattle would graze in the first pasture four times for each single rotation in the other pastures. My land had thirty acres of prime grass. The ranchers were not happy about losing my land as part of their lease.

My fence was going to be post and rail, and I had caught a break, because I bordered an eighteen-hundred-acre ranch and already had an existing fence on one side of the property. When I started building the fence, I heard I was about to be sued by some neighbors, and the race was on. We did posts first and then wired it closed. Sandy's cousin Paul, who worked on the family ranch, helped. The fence was weak, but it would work while the litigation took its course.

Some of my neighbors decided to take action because I was a Jew from New York, and they didn't think I should be able to own my property. They managed to manipulate the homeowners' association into paying for the lawsuit. In effect, I was suing myself. Property bordering mine was allowed to fence out the cows because their land was in a different filing. Some homeowners and, eventually, the Colorado Supreme Court felt that I had violated the covenants by trying to own my land. I managed to sweet-talk the neighboring rancher into haying my property. During the life of the fence, he managed to cut over eighty tons of hay off my land.

Today my litigation is taught at the Colorado University Law School and is required reading for anyone interested in Colorado subdivision law. I had played by all the rules, but, no matter the results, they were not going to let me own my property. The first case was a mixed result and left no one happy, especially since the first judge ruled that I couldn't sue myself and that the neighbors would be responsible for the court costs. The supreme court said I could sue myself but ruled against the subdivision with regard to the locked gate and who had legal access to the roads. It ruled on a new structure to use with regard to the cattle lease and who was responsible and where the funds should be spent.

The road and locked gate were a new phenomenon. The road used to be open for public access to the West Elk Wilderness Area boundary. When the community that won't admit it exists was formed, a locked gate appeared. The public was denied access, because neither the county nor the forest service would assume the responsibility of maintaining the road. The supreme court ruled that the only people with a legal right to drive on the road are the people who pay for the roads to be maintained, and that is the community that won't admit it exists.

When the developer bought the ranch, he divided the ranch into five different subdivisions, each with its own rules. As added value to sell lots, he allowed those subdivisions exclusive rights to access the wilderness area. The supreme court ruled that they could walk in to have fishing access but had no rights to drive on the roads.

Because of fear of further litigation, the rulings have never been enforced. The community that won't admit it exists doesn't care about its property rights. The community doesn't care if its money is mismanaged, if the land is abused by overgrazing, or if the ditches and land are not maintained. After all, the community's citizens are lucky to spend a couple of weeks there. They would finally get rid of the Jew from New York.

It would take twenty years to sell out, and, of course, I reached a settlement with the developer. It just shows that, when it comes to real estate, you can always find someone more ignorant than you. Someday, someone in the community will wake up and make some people miserable again. There are a few good people in Whistling Streams, but they are far outnumbered by the bad. There is litigation going on today, and it is neighbor against neighbor, suing over land and water rights they don't own. They would be better served to sue the homeowners' association and make a little money.

Ten

The Dos

The Dos Rios golf course hole number thirteen.

Colorado has many great golf courses, and the ball travels a lot farther there. Redlands Mesa, outside of Grand Junction and located at the base of the Colorado National Monument, is one of the prettiest. There are great courses in Aspen, Snowmass, Vail, Telluride, Ridgeway, Durango, and Delta.

The Dos Rios golf course is a par seventy-one; its front nine are not much, but its back nine are very pretty. It crosses both the Gunnison River and Tomichi Creek. Water can come into play on every hole of the back nine. It is not long and thus makes for a good grandpa course. It is located at an elevation of 7,700 feet, and your ball will travel around 15 percent farther than it will at sea level.

When I first played the Dos, it cost nine dollars to play nine holes. It had no back nine yet. My buddy Ralphie, who had worked on the roof of my new house, talked me into buying a set of clubs. He had won a set of Titleist irons in Delta and gave me a good deal on them. I started playing a little bit at a time. Finally King George, the general manager and greenskeeper, determined that I had to become a member. He said that the club had a rule that you couldn't play the course more than five times a year otherwise. The member initiation fee was $250, and annual dues were another $250. Because I wasn't happy about it, he waived the initiation fee, and I became a member.

One day I was playing with my good friends Juandando, Fondando, Zipper, and the Frogman. We were partying our way around the course. When we got to the par-three seventh tee box, Juandando pulled out a fat one. I hit last in the group. The tees were back, and so was the pin, and it was a 175-yard shot over water and into the strong wind. I pured a four iron, and it felt good. I couldn't see where it landed, but it had a good line.

We got to the green, and everyone found his ball, except me. My friends started cursing and helping me look for my ball. I thought my ball must have gone over the green and didn't think to look in the hole. Finally, after a few minutes, Juandando went to pull the pin so that he could putt. He found my ball in the hole. It was a perfect shot on an otherwise forgettable round. Zipper would tell everyone it had hit the bridge, ricocheted off a tree, and gone in. He never saw it, of course. I had to buy a few drinks and was happy to do so. It was front-page news in the *Gunnison Country Times*, and I had my first hole in one. I was happy about it but wished I could have seen it go in.

For those who say it is impossible to build a golf course for under a million dollars, I let them know about Dos Rios. Its front nine was built for $70,000. People volunteered time and equipment. When the back nine were built a dozen or so years later, it cost $250,000. Affordable golf can happen if enough people want to make it happen.

The back nine has quite a few single-family homes. A golf course definitely increases the value of a community. When my wife at the time was pregnant with our first child, she insisted that she was not going to carry a baby in and out of my house on snowshoes. We bought a beautiful home just off the eleventh green. The house was much larger and more luxurious than my place in Whistling Streams. It was a great house for my girls to grow up in.

I taught my girls the game of golf. They may not play the game now, but maybe someday they will enjoy it. When they were little, I took them golf-ball hunting. Every spring, when the snow and ice would melt off the course, was our prime golf-ball-hunting time. My friend Yonkale would agree with the fact that finding golf balls can be more fun than playing the game. We would find hundreds. We would clean them up, and the girls would set up in the backyard, usually during the member-guest tournament, and sell balls for a quarter each. They did OK, but one year they got greedy. They made their operation self-service and would leave the balls and the money on a table with a sign. Well, the members of Dos Rios are honorable people, and no one ripped them off. I did get a complaint from the pro shop and had to shut down the girls' operation.

The membership of Dos Rios was around 150 people, and I had some great times at the club. The club used to have a swimming pool. The kids loved to swim there and were hard to get out of the pool. After a tragic accident, the club decided the pool was not worth it and closed it. I always liked the pool and was sorry to see it close, but I understood the decision.

Men's league was on Thursday nights, and usually people would get off work early and make a day of it. Men's league is a team match-play competition. I played on lots of different teams over the years, but my favorite was Ralphie's team. We never won the championship but came close a couple of times. Half a Ton of Fun was the powerhouse team back in the day, and they were an intimidating bunch. After the matches, we would barbecue steaks and drink beer. Thursday nights we would hear all about what was going on in the area; it was better than reading the local papers.

I played in tournaments once in a while. When Skyland was built, we had another course to play on. Skyland is located just outside of Crested Butte and is a world-class facility. The course itself was built and designed by Robert Trent Jones Jr. and is a par seventy-two. Skyland went bankrupt several times and today goes by the name of Crested Butte Country Club. I would play in the member-versus-member tournament called the Home and Home every chance I could. Even though the Crested Butte course was much longer and more difficult, Gunnison members would routinely win the event. During one Home and Home, I shot my best round ever at Skyland: an eighty-five. The next day I was paired with Ralphie, and we had to play against the Crested Butte club pro and the head greenskeeper. The greenskeeper was a nice guy, but the club pro was arrogant and the last person you wanted to play against. The club pro wanted to play from the back tees. The tournament rules stated that the matches were to be played from the front tees, unless the whole group agreed to the move. Well, the club pro called me every sissy name in the book, but we would play from the front tees. The fronts had been moved back anyway, but the club pro was beaten before the match started. Back then I had around a twenty handicap, so I got a lot of strokes. On number five, the number-one handicap hole, the club pro had a tap-in birdie, but somehow I made a forty-foot putt for par and net eagle and won the hole. The club pro was furious and took it out on his partner. When Ralphie pulled the same thing on number thirteen and made a net eagle, the match was over.

I would sometimes play in the Fall Classic, which again had one round in Crested Butte and one round in Gunnison. My oldest nephew was visiting, and he is a decent golfer, even if he is slower than molasses. The format was a two-man best ball, and our first round was up in Crested Butte. My nephew played lights-out and shot an eighty-two. I would better his score on only two holes, and we shot a net eighty—good enough to lead the second flight. I had two good friends playing in the tournament from the Dos, and the "Wathead" and the "Droid" had a strategy. The field was divided after the first round; my friend's strategy was to play as badly as possible in Crested Butte and get in the last flight so that they could shoot lights-out on their home course. Their strategy worked for them multiple times. My nephew got loaded after the first round and wound up getting sick out the window on the way home. The next day he was rather hung over and a shadow of his former self, and I would carry us to victory on my home course; we shot a net seventy-eight. My buddies shot a net seventy and had the round of the day.

For people not familiar with golf, the term "sandbagger" needs to be explained. A sandbagger is someone who reports all his bad scores and forgets about some of the good scores. He winds up with a higher handicap than he should. A lot of people thought I was a sandbagger. I would shoot more bad rounds than good, depending on my mood and sobriety. The Dos has lots of sandbaggers, but my idol was Okie. Okie was fun to play with and was always upbeat. He always played—no matter who the opponent—just good enough to win, and, yes, he got enough strokes. Okie was a retired air-force colonel and has passed away, but he brought sandbagging to an art form.

The premier event at the Dos was the Dos Rios Open, a match-play format that happens the first weekend in August. Flights were determined by handicap, and I almost always played in the last flight. One year I played a semifinal match against Gumber, a summer resident from Texas who, in his prime, was a good golfer and had played in money matches with Ben Hogan. It was a tough match, with a lot of back and forth. I really don't like "Texicans." We got to number sixteen, the longest and last par five, all square. I was walking, and he was riding a cart. After our tee shots, we set off to hit our second shots. I hadn't hit a good drive and was in the rough; Gumber had hit a perfect drive and was in the fairway. For some reason, Gumber drove up to my ball and looked at it. It had a bad lie in the rough. I slowed down my walking pace, and sure enough, he pulled out a club and hit a fantastic shot just short of the green. I suppressed a smile as I walked up to his ball. I looked at the ball and announced that the ball was not mine. Gumber knew he screwed up, and he knew the rules of golf, but that didn't stop him from trying to sweet-talk me. "But I hit a fantastic shot," he said.

"I know," I replied, and I could contain my smile no longer. He asked if he could get my ball and put it where it had been moments ago. The penalty for hitting the wrong ball in match play is loss of hole. He knew the rule but was hoping I didn't. "No," I said, "you lose the hole."

Angry, he turned away from me. It was the turning point in the match. We pushed on seventeen, and on eighteen I managed to sink a ten-foot bogey putt to halve the hole and win the match one up. I went on to win the final match and won the grandpa flight that year. The match against Gumber, though, ranks number one with me as best of all time.

One year I wanted to play in the Dos and went to register at the pro shop. GJ was the club pro back then and said fine, but that I couldn't play in the last flight. I asked why not. He said I had won too many times. (I had won last flight a couple of times.) I tried to sweet-talk GJ and be persuasive, but he insisted I move up a flight. I wouldn't stand a chance in the next flight, because it had even better sandbaggers. I haven't played in the Dos in a long time since.

The most fun event at the Dos was the Pasta Open. It is no longer held, because GJ moved up to the Butte. The Pasta Open was a team scramble event, and the best thing about the tournament was the food served after the round. One year GJ invited some friends of his from Denver to play in the Pasta Open. They owned a popular golf store in Denver. The Pasta Open was a shotgun start. I called GJ to find out where to start, and he told me to go to the twelfth tee. I was happy, because that was close to the house. The new basketball coach at the college was the only other local in our small group. We had the smallest group in the tournament that year, but I know we had the most fun.

What had happened was that GJ's friends from Denver had showed up in Gunnison with a couple of hookers. The girls didn't play, but whenever they got bored or wanted attention, they removed articles of clothing. They weren't bad-looking either. We passed a group of locals led by Nelson the bartender, and I waved and shouted greetings. The next thing I knew, the girls decide to flash Nelson's group. Nelson was not going to be outdone. He got his group to line up and pull down their pants, flashing the girls the moon right back.

As we approached our last hole, the eleventh, I began to worry about the girls doing something stupid on my home green. I prayed my future ex would not be looking out the window. Sure enough, one of the girls got naked and sat down with her legs spread around the hole. What a target to putt at! I don't think I reached the hole on my first try. My future ex never looked out the window that day. As far as a fun day on the golf course, it has been hard to beat the Pasta Open that year.

I had one more hole in one at the Dos, and again it was on number seven. I was playing a five-dollar Nassau with another summer resident from Pueblo. A great guy off the course, he had a tendency to be obnoxious on the course. It was after my holy hole in one in Israel. I have been lucky enough to have three holes in one, but the last one was the best, because I actually got to see the ball go in the hole. For anyone who plays golf, a hole in one is a big deal. A lot of good golfers and pros have never had one. Well, after the ball went in, I looked at my playing partner, and he was shaking his head and told me that it's only one hole. Not even "Nice shot" or "Congrats"—just "It's only one hole." In a way he was right, because I won the hole and the front nine, but he came back to win the back, and I lost five dollars.

I have witnessed only one other hole in one in my life. The one the Rolling Stones' lawyer made on number fifteen at Key Biscayne in Florida doesn't count, because he hit a shot in the water first, and there is no such thing as a mulligan hole in one. The one I witnessed was during men's league on number twelve. We were playing against Half a Ton of Fun. Mallard was a real nice guy who grew up in Gunnison and could hit the ball a long way. He liked to call me Oscar, after the character in the *Six Million Dollar Man* who has the same last name as me. Anyway, after Mallard made his hole in one, he had a smile on his face, but his eyes were sad. I asked him what was wrong. He asked me if I was going to tell anyone. First of all, it's men's league, and there are around a hundred golfers on the course. After the round, there was a barbecue and drinks. I answered that of course and I was going tell everyone, and it was really going to cost him. We could never beat Half a Ton of Fun. That cheapskate chicken-poop Mallard would not show his face in the clubhouse after the round, because he didn't want to buy everyone drinks, as tradition demands.

The Dos is one of the places that make the Gunnison country special. Over the years, it has been a place of refuge and many good times. With the exception of men's league and tournaments, I don't take golf too seriously. The Dos and its members have done much for their community. I would be happy if the club I hope to build is like the Dos.

Eleven
CD Inc.

The Sound Factor was still struggling along when we decided to move our location. Our landlord had changed, and he wanted more rent. We found a building for sale, one block south and still on Main Street, between the W café and a summer restaurant called Johnson's. For whatever reason, our business improved greatly with the new location. Being on the first block of Main Street made a difference.

It was not long after our move that Alin and Sandy began having problems with their marriage and eventually divorced. I think Alin would have been happy to stay married, but Sandy was miserable. Once the divorce was final, Alin wanted to leave town. I bought his share of the business and building. Although Alin misrepresented the amount of debt the business had, I was happy with the deal. Alin moved on to San Diego and was not heard from again. Sandy would eventually marry a county commissioner and move to Crested Butte. She definitely stepped up in class.

To me, if a business is not growing, it might as well be dead. I changed the product mix and got rid of the esoteric brands and focused more on affordable products. Around that time, videocassette recorders became affordable, and their prices would keep falling in the future. Movies began to be released on videotapes, and the Sound Factor became Gunnison's first movie-rental business. I charged ten dollars to rent the machine and five dollars for a movie. After a year, I had competition, and not long after, the grocery store City Market would get into the business, and prices would drop to three dollars a movie.

We had a small selection of movies compared to the big video stores that opened. At most, I carried a couple of hundred titles. I had a half dozen dirty movies that I kept under the counter. I could have made a lot more money with dirty movies, but I wasn't into porn, and it was a small town.

One day a high-school kid came into the store and told me his mom had asked him to pick up a couple of dirty movies. Well, I knew the kid, and he was a great golfer. As a senior he won the state high-school championship. Anyway, I let him rent a couple of dirty movies, which was a mistake. The next day the mom (daughter of a Gunnison bank owner) came into the store, and she was mighty angry with me for renting her son a couple of dirty movies. When she asked me why I had rented them to him, I told her that her son had told me the movies were for her. Well, that made her madder. She was right, though, and I never rented a movie to someone underage again.

I used to have a lot of friends in Lake City. Lake City is a beautiful, remote mountain town sixty miles from Gunnison. It has a year-round population of a few hundred people but has no supermarket. One day a lovely lady by the name of Sue came into the Sound Factor. She had just opened a secondhand clothing store in her house, and she wanted to get in the video-rental business. Of course she had no funds, but she had a location. I liked Sue and trusted her, so I agreed to her proposal, and Lake City had its first video-rental business. I would eventually make as much money from her business as I did from my own. She had no competition.

With the break up of AT&T, their monopoly on the phone business ended. People now had to buy their own phones, and that presented a new business opportunity for the Sound Factor. I became an AT&T phone center and sold lots of telephone products. The phone business was good, and I thought opening up phone centers in other small mountain towns might be a good idea.

I figured a service business would be an asset for the shop. I could give someone space for free, and he could keep whatever money he made in repairs there. I figured that whatever was broken and too expensive to fix would lead to a sale for me. I also thought the store would be more customer-friendly with its own service department.

My first technician wound up in jail and then had to leave town. The second one was the one I liked the best of the three I tried out. He was an air-force-trained technician and would actually work. I called him a "yutz." I have no idea what a *yutz* is or if it's even a word, but I meant it as a term of friendship. The yutz wanted to make more money (he had a couple of kids to support) and eventually moved on to Grand Junction.

Marky was a Jehovah Witness and was young, ambitious, and not a bad salesman for a technician. Marky thought the phone business was great and decided to go into the commercial-phone business. Marky had a friend in Salida already in the business, and when he came to the store, he also wanted to open AT&T phone centers in Salida and Alamosa. I agreed to work with him but soon developed a lack of trust and shut the stores off after a couple of months. Eventually Marky made enough money selling phone systems that he gave up on repairing hi-fi equipment and had to move out. He made enough in his business for a down payment on a ranch. Eventually he went broke and left the county.

My home builder, Mr. B, also liked the idea of selling phones and, since he had family in Glenwood Springs, wanted to partner for a store there. Mr. B's dad lived in Glenwood, so he had a free place to live there. Glenwood is a much higher class of small town than Gunnison was, and expenses were higher. We never made any money there and closed the store after a year and a half. I learned that being bigger does not guarantee that you will make more profit. Growth without profit is meaningless.

The Sound Factor was a fun place to hang out. Aside from a lot of toys to play with, I had a chessboard set up on the counter. I am not a great chess player, but I enjoy the game and am not terrible at it. Eventually I had a group of buddies who would come in just to play chess. When it was slow, it was fun to play. When it was busy, it was impossible to play.

A lot of people credit Sony and its Walkman for being the first portable personal-listening device. But a few years before the Walkman appeared, there was Astral Tunes. Astral Tunes, a company out of Salt Lake City, made the first personal-listening device. They manufactured none of the components, which were easy to knock off. A Denver distributor put together its own version, and I sold quite a few. The device was a car stereo that used a nickel-cadmium rechargeable battery as its power source. The car stereo had a headphone jack, and the unit came with cheap Sennheiser headphones. It also came with a small carrying pack. Definitely not pocket-sized, the product was originally designed for skiers to take on the slopes. The unit was hardly lightweight, and if you crashed the wrong way, it would definitely leave a mark. Sony's Walkman revolutionized portable electronics, but Astral Tunes developed the concept.

Compact discs first appeared in the marketplace in 1984, and by 1985 Technics had introduced its first compact-disc player. The Sound Factor was the largest Technics account on the western slope of Colorado, and so I got into the CD business. Not much music existed on compact disc. Telarc was the largest compact-disc seller at the outset, and they sold mostly classical music.

At around the time of my first daughter's birth, one of my suppliers started to complain about his business. He owned Cable of America, and I bought Akai products and speaker wire and Maxell tapes from Cable. When Mitsubishi bought

Akai, Cable lost its main line, as the Akai brand would disappear from America. I told Gene to get into the CD business, as it was bound to explode.

Gene was of mixed decent: his father was Japanese, and his mother was Italian. His father was sent to an internment camp during World War II. Gene looked Japanese and had a Japanese last name. He fought and was wounded in the Korean War as a marine-corps officer. Gene is as tough as nails when he has to be.

Gene didn't want to go into the CD business by himself but saw the potential. He asked me to be his partner. My first daughter was born, and I wanted to make more money. I decided to liquidate the Sound Factor and go into business with Gene in Denver. Our new business was called CD Inc.

Panasonic owns the Technics brand, and back then Denver had its own distribution center. They didn't want to lose me as an account. Panasonic Denver was like a family to me, and I knew everyone who worked there. Originally, a company called Newcraft was the rep and distributor for Denver. The head of Panasonic credit would become a close friend, and he was in shock about me going into business with Gene. Ross, the credit manager, said he never met two people more opposite in business together. Technics had only one distributor in the United States at the time, and he mostly dealt in refurbished products. They made CD Inc. a key dealer and gave us additional discounts on their products. In three short years, CD Inc. went from zero sales to over a million dollars a year selling Technics-branded products. Cable (Gene's company) had a similar arrangement with JVC, but Cable never came close to our sales with Technics.

The folks at JVC didn't like me much, and that was fine with me. The folks at Panasonic never really liked Gene. We were in the CD market, but our business with Panasonic would always be more profitable. When we started our business, there were six major labels that distributed most of the music sold in America—PolyGram, RCA, Capitol, MCA, Warner Brothers, and CBS— and all would eventually allow us to distribute their products.

Back then there was doubt about the viability of compact discs as a real product. Capitol Records had only twenty-five titles available on compact disc when we started doing business. One title was *Dark Side of the Moon*, which would be our all-time best-selling title. Our market was hi-fi dealers who were selling CD players and needed to sell discs, because a lot of record stores didn't sell compact discs yet. We sold to independent record stores as well.

Our first home run with compact discs came when we convinced the Denver-based SoundTrack chain to sell discs. They had nine stores around the Denver area. We sold them racks and stocked them with over a hundred titles. SoundTrack liked Gene, but Gene didn't know anything about music, so I had the responsibility of managing and servicing each store. Dennis was the operations manager, and if you could keep him on the phone for more than fifteen seconds, it was a major accomplishment. A typical conversation with Dennis was very short, and he spoke quicker than anyone I have ever known. Dennis would give me my purchase-order numbers, and he thought SoundTrack had more discs stolen than sold. I don't know about that, but SoundTrack was a good account and helped our credibility with the record labels. SoundTrack eventually went public as Ultimate Electronics. Ultimate rapidly grew to over sixty stores and then went bankrupt. It resurfaced out of bankruptcy for a little while and then went bankrupt again and is no longer in business today.

Our first year in business, we set up at the Consumer Electronics Show in Las Vegas. You have to remember that the viability of compact discs was still in doubt. CES is a huge event, and in Vegas, it is its second-largest trade show. Our territory went from Montana south to El Paso and west to Idaho. We had dealers show up at our booth. After this show, CD Inc. became an international company. One person who showed up in our booth was a real character. His badge read "Nate"—and I'm not even going to try and spell his last name—"Panasonic Company."

I knew Nate, and this dude was not Nate, so naturally I was on red alert. Nate ran Technics in the Los Angeles area and would rise to run the western region for Panasonic Company. I called him out, and he introduced himself as Doug with an obviously Jewish last name. Dougie worked for New West Audio out of Burbank, California. He bought a couple of discs that day. He would become the soul of CD Inc.'s Technics business.

Doug's company represented RAMSA products in the LA region. RAMSA was Panasonic's commercial sound division. You might have heard of one of his customers: Guitar Center. Doug's company couldn't buy Technics from Nate. Try as he might, Doug couldn't buy from Nate's company, but Nate allowed me to sell him. We sold more Technics 1200MKII turntables than any account in America. When Technics sold DAT machines, we would also sell the most. Eventually the Technics brand would disappear from the audio business. But it still markets the 1200 turntable and kept Guitar Center as an account; last I heard, they were buying eight hundred a month.

Panasonic owns RAMSA, and they mostly sold speakers for commercial applications. RAMSA is on the industrial side of Panasonic. Back then one side of the company did not deal with the other. We established a network of all the RAMSA reps across the country and sold them Technics products. It was a perfect network to sell into, because the product never really showed up at consumer retail.

CD Inc. made money its first year in business, as the annual sales were close to a million dollars. CD Inc.'s sales were greater than Cable's from year one—not bad for a brand-new company. Gene and his wife did all the administration for CD Inc. They hated the work and really didn't like music. They had to enter over a thousand titles on the computer and keep track of them all. They moaned and groaned a lot. Gene could not complain about the results, and I know CD Inc.'s success surprised him.

Pace membership warehouse stores were our next home run. Pace was a warehouse club based down the street from our warehouse. After a long courtship, Pace agreed to buy compact discs from CD Inc. They had over thirty stores across America at the time, and their opening order was rather large. Gene had a lot more work. I think Pace drove Gene over the edge, in the end.

Creating product for Pace was my job, and Pace could sell a lot of products. I created custom box sets to build a ticket and sell more products per SKU number. I was limited to twenty SKUs per store. Suddenly no one at the labels was disputing CD Inc.'s credibility. I got tickets to any concert I wanted in Denver, including backstage passes and a barbecue with Don Henley. The music business had the best perks once upon a time.

111

CD Inc. would grow as long as Gene could handle it. When Stanton Electronics introduced a dual compact disc player, I went to visit my oldest sister, Esta, in New York. Stanton was based in Plainview, New York, which is the town she lived in. Stanton was one of America's largest phono cartridge makers. Its 680ee is the gold standard for most DJs. When it launched the dual CD, it also introduced a line of mixers. When I met Jack, who was son-in-law of the company founder, I told him about my business. Jack appointed me his factory rep for the Rocky Mountain region. I had become my father's son without the help of my family.

Twelve

The Fall

Pace was CD Inc.'s largest account; it sold a lot of compact discs. The problem was that, when they paid the bill, they would take an arbitrary deduction. It was never more than 2 percent, but it made Gene crazy. In addition, there were returns. I obviously tried to pick the best-selling product for them, but I wasn't perfect, and consequently we would have returns. The labels would take back any overstocked inventory we had. But to Gene, returns were another administrative nightmare and more work. Pace was opening around four new stores a year, and they wanted money from their suppliers for each new store opening. If we had been a larger company, it would not have been a problem. Gene hated the idea of giving cash allowances for each new store opening. Every dollar we made was important to us.

Pace would eventually be bought and absorbed by Sam's Club. When they wanted to buy a massive number of the *Batman* videos from us, Gene went over the edge and wanted out of the business. Gene never liked or understood the music business. Selling equipment was much cleaner, simpler, and more profitable. But most importantly, it was child's play to administer.

I know Gene never expected CD Inc. to grow into what it had. Sometimes we would have monthly bills of more than a quarter of a million dollars. Gene felt the stress more than I did, because he was writing the checks and managing our cash flow. Somehow we always paid our bills on time. But Gene couldn't take it anymore and wanted out of the business. He tried to sell his company and his half of the interest in CD Inc.

At the same time that Gene was having his meltdown, my home life was falling apart. My wife wanted a divorce, and she wanted half my money. She never supported me in my business and felt I didn't need to work. I would commute to Denver early Monday morning and return home Thursday evening. It was brutal, but she sure liked spending the money I earned. We had lived together for six years, and during that time, we'd had a warm, loving relationship. Aside from Australia and New Zealand, I took her to Hamadia. She loved Israel and cried when we left. She said she could live there, but I knew it would never happen. We traveled to the Virgin Islands—the most expensive trip I would ever take. We had a special place on the ocean in Laguna Beach that we would often visit.

When she became pregnant with our first child, the relationship totally changed. Our marriage was a joke, and it would last four years. We had no wedding or honeymoon, and I can count on one hand the amount of times we made love since our marriage. The birth of our second daughter was a miracle. I still didn't want a divorce; I felt maybe she could change again. Esta was not right about many things, but she was right about my ex.

A lot of people never understood how a yippie could be partners with an ex-marine officer. I needed Gene; Gene would teach me a lot about business and life. Gene gave me strength and confidence. I never had to worry about the details of business as long as Gene was my partner. Gene had his network of small dealers throughout the Rocky Mountain region. His company was a great one-man operation, and, with CD Inc. paying its share of the expenses, it was always profitable. He sold mostly JVC products (car and home stereo) and some other junk. When JVC came to him with a refurbished list, his business became interesting.

I always felt I had a special relationship with Panasonic, and I would do favors for them. They closed the Denver warehouse, and products then came from Cypress, California. Sales responsibility for our region was shifted to San Francisco. Before Denver was shut down, I helped them with their telephone products. For some reason, they had problems making their sales quota. They did have many calls from outside the territory, but they could not ship outside their territory. Someone decided (not me) that maybe Bill could help us out. We would get paid 2 percent of the nut. We would be paid when the product hit our door, and the customers would pay all freight charges from Denver. We now had customers in New York City, Miami, Paraguay, and Belgium.

Gene's biggest account was in Houston, Texas. Leader Marketing was a road-show operation. They would set up in all the major cities across the country, doing weekend liquidation sales. Gene sold them a lot of JVC-refurbished product. In spite of himself, Gene would do big-time volume for JVC. Panasonic phone business accounts gave Gene an international market for his refurbished video cameras.

I guess what people don't get is that Gene treated me like dog poop. He milked CD Inc. for expenses yet never compensated the company for his added business. Gene hardly paid me anything out of Cable. Gene did take care of me at our annual trade shows. Gene would want me to gamble with him in Vegas, and Cable would always pay for our trips there. That was it.

I didn't think Gene could find a buyer for his business. I did find someone who was willing to buy Gene out of CD Inc., and so, on an experimental basis, he took the Tuna's money. The Tuna owned one of the most-successful independent record stores in Denver. The Tuna operated in a gray area of the music business, and he bought products from all the label reps. The thing was that it was promotional product not technically for sale. He would repackage the brand-new product and sell it as used. Some labels gave him catalog product, and he could order just like a direct account. The Tuna knew way more about the music business than I did, and he was better connected.

I let the Tuna pick a Pace title, and he chose *Elvis's Top Ten Hits*, a two-CD package. He also negotiated a great price with RCA. Well, we ordered a thousand copies, and when they hit our warehouse, Gene hit the roof. He could not believe that Pace would sell through on Elvis and that we would have to return most of the product. He thought the product would not sell at retail. Elvis was dead, and so Gene wanted to bet the Tuna a lobster dinner. They made the bet, but Gene never paid his obligation to the Tuna. He should have thought about of how cheap we bought the product and how much extra profit we would make.

Pace would not sell a thousand copies of Elvis; it sold two thousand. When I went to visit the New West Audio boys in La Costa, California, Gene would have his chance to terminate the experiment. The Tuna was a bigger slob than me and dressed like he was homeless. The Tuna could be meaner and nastier than Gene. The Tuna also had a temper to boot. The Tuna started by questioning what CD Inc. was paying Cable for overhead. Gene lost his temper, and it almost came to blows. As tough as Gene was, the Tuna had nothing to worry about, as he could easily have wiped the floor with Gene. The Tuna, to his credit, did not beat up Gene before he left. He did threaten him, and Gene was scared. Gene called me in California and told me the experiment was over. The Tuna would get his money back, and Gene had ruined my day.

Gene told me it's easy to sell product to someone who isn't going to pay you. Well, CD Inc. was fortunate, and it was very rare for someone to stiff us. Leader Marketing was going bankrupt, and Gene had been warned. The buyer assured Gene that he saw a check made out to Cable and that it was going out. Cable wound up being burned for twenty-five thousand dollars, and worse was that I was the new owner of Cable and would have to absorb the loss.

Gene had found a buyer for his business: some guy who used to work for Sharp. This time I didn't like the guy and, in hindsight, should have liquidated the business right then and there. But I agreed to buy Gene out—my ego got the best of me, plus Gene said he would stay on and work for a couple of years. Gene's buddy wound up going into business with the Sony rep, but it wouldn't last long at all. I knew deep down that the days of explosive growth and making good money was over. It would take a few years to wind down the business and liquidate.

CD Inc. was at the right place at the right time with the right product. I worked hard and learned much about business. I love music and had fun in the business, even though it wasn't as profitable as electronics. In the end, Gene was out for himself, just like my ex. If I had to do it over again, I wouldn't do it. The bottom line was that business became the least of my worries because of my problems at home. I would eventually lose all desire to make money. After Gene left the business, I never spoke to him again. I imagine he is happy and still gambling.

Back home I was going through hell. I think divorce is worse than death. For me, divorce meant I was a failure. How much money I made or could make lost all importance. I lost all interest in people, both family and friends. I had failed at the most important relationship of my life.

My two daughters became the most important things in my life. I would be a weekend dad, and once in a while get to show them other places in the world. I could never vent my anger or frustration at their mother, because it would only hurt them. I couldn't explain to them the agony I felt every time I brought them back to their mother. The teachers at school could not believe my kids had divorced parents. They did great in school and had many friends. The fact that they grew up happy was a miracle and a blessing. Their father just sank deeper and deeper into the depths of depression.

I remember the song "Nobody Knows You" that we had to learn and sing at Camp Roosevelt. No one wants to deal with negativity in one's life. The adages such as just deal with it, move on, time heals all wounds, get a life, quit feeling sorry for yourself—that should have been enough to get me moving again, but it wasn't.

The money I lost and the folding of my business were irrelevant to me. I could not care less about material possessions. What was destroying me was my failure as a person. I thought I knew a couple of people and tried to love them, but the experience had shown me I could never trust again. I would make a few attempts, but I would never want to live with another woman again. I would never wish my experience on anyone else. For some people, divorce is a good thing, and their lives are bettered. For me, it was a tragedy that will haunt me every day of my life. Some families, like Esta's, seem miserable. They are constantly fighting, screaming, and cursing at one another. But at the end of the day, they loved one another. No matter how miserable they made one another, they at least had love. I was just miserable.

It would take a close friend's death sentence to get me to start thinking about life again. My kids were not kids anymore, and the last thing they wanted to do was hang out with their dad in the middle of nowhere. They no longer needed me, and that was fine. They were happy, and that was important.

The Beatles sang, "And in the end, the love you take is equal to the love you make." Chumbawamba sang, "You only get what you give." Neither has been my experience. It sounds like it should work, in theory. But most people are selfish and have no clue about giving. For me, giving (and I am not talking about materially) is natural, and I enjoy trying to help people. I can dream that someday I will get what I gave.

The Zipper was one of my closest Gunnison friends. When he was diagnosed with inoperable cancer, it shook me up. He had everything to live for: a great family and a great life. Some things in life are beyond our control, and so, it seems, is one's death.

He grew up in Niagara Falls, New York, and went to school at Western, at least for a little while. He built his own business in floor coverings but specialized in tile. He was a successful and driven person. His best buddy was the Frog, and the two of them had their own language and were hysterical together. Each had twenty different nicknames for the other.

We would all play poker together on Thursday nights, next to the town's mortuary across from the police station. Our games were wild and could get out of control quickly. My buddy Mr. B used to say that if it had been the Wild West, I would have been shot dead. I don't know if I was cheating, but I used to like to look at my neighbor's cards. I was obvious about it, and nobody ever enjoyed sitting next to me at a poker game.

None of our games would get violent, except once, when I wanted to punch the lights out of the little Zipper. He must have thought I was bluffing, and he got burnt on a good-size pot. He stood up and threw his cards in my face. Well, the drinks kind of scattered as I lunged across the table, and after some loud bellowing noises, we calmed down. I never landed my punch, and we remained good friends.

I can be a pretty annoying person when I want to be, especially on the golf course. The Zipper never accepted my hole in one as a good shot. We played some golf together, but only nine holes, as he would feel guilty and always had to be someplace else. At poker games, he always had to leave to be home by eleven. He never rocked the boat at home and was always there on time.

His daughter was the same age as my youngest, and we went to a lot of the same school functions. He was a good dad, but his daughter was a handful. We sure shared a lot of laughs and special times, and I still think of him often.

My little buddy's illness made me hunger for another adventure. They say you can't go home again, but I would try. Israel was a totally different country than the one I left in 1975. For one thing, there was a wave of Russian immigration after the fall of Communism. The country was a lot more affluent and developed. The Socialists were no longer in charge, and most kibbutzniks lived on the bottom of the scale instead of the top. The second intifada was just starting when I arrived in October 2000.

My plan was to go back to school and improve my Hebrew. My Hebrew was at a first-grade level, and if I wanted to find an opportunity in Israel, I would have to better my vocabulary. I decided to move into the Park Hotel and study at Ulpan Akiva in Netanya. Instead of working half a day, I would play golf in Caesarea.

Thirteen

Golf in Israel

This is the best golfer ever produced in Israel and the current women's national champion.

Golfing in Israel is a little different than golfing in America. Its people are what make it so special and unique. Golf would become my escape and source for fun. What better place to meet people? The more I studied the language, the better I would be able to communicate.

My Ulpan class was mostly Russian and mostly ladies; it was a different and more serious class than the one I went to in Hamadia. Grammar in the Hebrew language is not simple stuff, and Ulpan Akiva helped my grammar a lot. My Hebrew advanced, and suddenly I could listen to the news on the radio or watch it on TV and understand the dialogue. My reading was weak, but even that improved.

I had played Caesarea back in 1982, when I visited with my ex. The old course was a long and difficult par seventy-three. It was located about two miles from the Mediterranean Sea, and that's usually where the prevailing winds came from. Golf in Israel is different than anywhere in the world, because mostly Israelis play there. I like to describe Israelis as New Yorkers on steroids.

On Saturday mornings at Caesarea, they still play the KC. Named after Katz and Cubernik, the KC was a foursome's competition, where the two best scores counted in a Stableford scoring system. Sounds complicated, huh? Back then, Jules and Mike still played. Jules was from Pittsburgh and flew B17 bombers during World War II. He was a crusty old dog and loved to give everyone a hard time. The KC is partly named for him. Mike is from South Africa and is a pussycat. It's hard to describe Mike, other than to say he is mostly bald with a face you would remember if you saw it. Mike still shows up at the KC and distributes the numbered cards that determine who is on your team and when and where you tee off. I can still hear his rasping half scream of "Kads," which signified the KC was about to begin. Aside from having a face only a mother could love, Mike used to work for the Ford Motor Company. I always enjoyed playing with Mike, even though he was a member of the South African mafia in Caesarea.

Moshe is another nice guy who was in charge of handicaps at Caesarea. He said I had to have a handicap to play and asked me what my handicap was. Because of the length and difficulty of the course, I figured I was a twenty-two. I joined the Israel Golf Federation and played to a twenty-two. After I won a couple of tournaments, Moshe lowered my handicap to eighteen, and when I won another tournament, it went down to sixteen, and I never won another tournament. Moshe spouted some nonsense about handicap being about potential to par. Last time I checked, handicap should be an average of one's last ten scores in relation to par. No way was I sixteen or an eighteen on that course, but Moshe was all-powerful, and so I had to play with the handicap given to me. Moshe is very much involved today in Caesarea, and I hear he has his own parking space.

Andy from Gilroy, California, is the club pro, and he played his college golf at San Jose State. Andy met his wife in Israel and decided to stay. He is not Jewish, and back then he was afraid to speak Hebrew. Andy's laid-back style is in contrast to the members, who are far from laid-back and kvetch constantly. Andy still runs the Caesarea golf operation and has come a long way. He is no longer afraid to speak Hebrew, and I believe he is happy.

Playing in the KC Saturday mornings was fun for me, and I got to meet a lot of people, because I never played in the same group twice. Unlike men's league, the KC allowed women and kids to play. The current national champion, Assaf, used to play in the KC. His dad is a good golfer as well as a former national champion. His dad used to be the mayor of the neighboring town of Or Akiva and taught many Israelis the game. Assaf wasn't bad back then and better than a lot of the men playing in the KC. I always enjoyed playing with him and the other kids in the KC. Assaf stressed about turning thirteen and moving back to the white tees. These days, I don't think he stresses about much when he plays golf.

Some folks from the Baha'i temple in Haifa used to play in the KC, and they were not great golfers. Charlie, who worked for the CIA, was a good golfer from St. Louis and fun to play with. Hedva was fine off the course, but on the course she was terrible. Bibi's favorite cousin played and would have a few good holes but was mostly an adventure to play with, although he was a very nice guy. Phillip was from Belgium and a good golfer and a real gentleman. I am glad the KC is still alive today.

On the old course, they used to have winter rules. In the States, winter rules meant that, if you had a bad lie in the fairway, you could move the ball no closer to the hole. In Israel, winter rules meant you could move the ball the length of a scorecard anywhere on the course, except on the green. I don't know if they still play winter rules on the fancy new course. I am sure the Royal and Ancient club would frown on such a rule. Any rule that makes the game easier works for me.

The intifada continued to grow in intensity, and people were dying almost every day. One day I decided to visit Hamadia, and on the way I saw a car being pulled over by the police in Wadi Ara. Wadi Ara is not in the West Bank but part of original Israel and contains many Arab villages.

When I got to Hamadia, I met with Yoav, and he was curious as to how I got to Hamadia. I told him I drove through Wadi Ara, and he said that was impossible, because the road was closed. What had happened was the car I saw being pulled over by the police had blown itself up, killing the occupants and two policeman. I had missed the explosion by a minute. On my way home after the road reopened, I saw hundreds of squashed paper cups, which were used to wash the blood off the road.

Hamadia was a shadow of its former self. It was struggling under a debt equivalent to thirty-two million dollars. A lot of the members I knew left. Yoav took me on a tour to the new border crossing, with Jordan and the new National Park built around the old spring where I had tried to put the moves on his sister-in-law. We went to lunch. That was the only meal the kibbutz still served, and now the members had to pay for food. The dream of the original pioneers was fading into meaninglessness. It was all very sad, but I still had friends who lived there.

The Ulpan was a challenge, but, after class was finished, I would head twelve miles away to Caesarea. One morning in class, almost everyone's phone went off at the same time. Netanya was a target throughout the length of the intifada. It was probably the second-most-violent city in Israel, with Jerusalem being the most attacked city in Israel. Tulkarm was only twelve miles away and the major jump-off point for attacks on Netanya. That morning, someone blew himself up at the entrance of the *canyon* (*canyon* is the Hebrew word for shopping mall). I can't remember the exact death toll, but it was more than a dozen. Galit, who is now the general manager of the Caesarea Golf Club, lost her mother-in-law that morning. The canyon would be bombed several more times during the length of the intifada.

I got to meet and play golf with many famous Israelis. Amos was one of my favorites. A retired major general and ex–Mirage fighter pilot, he is an older gentleman who likes golf. You know some people are special because of the twinkle in their eyes. Amos most definitely has a twinkle in his eyes. I never asked a lot of questions about people in Caesarea;

there was always a lot of other things to talk about. Amos learned his golf swing from Assaf's father. It was not a pretty swing, but Amos could hit it a long way on occasion. He told me about his visit to Telluride, and when I told him about Whistling Streams, I don't think he believed me.

Amos's best buddy was Yonkale, and they were a riot together. One day I played through Yonkale and Amos, and, instead of hitting my own ball, I hit Yonkale's. I made par and looked at the ball—oops. I gave Yonkale back his ball at the clubhouse. Yonkale and Amos are still good friends of mine.

Yoram turned out to be a major television personality and ex–rock star. I had no clue when I first played with him. Back then we were competitive but would always finish tied. The Japanese love ties, because no one loses face. Yoram has improved his game, and I am sure he would kick my butt today.

Simon would not be happy I mentioned his name in my story. Sorry, I am using his English name, and he is my most favorite member to play with at Caesarea. Simon likes to keep a low profile. He used to play with his buddy Yair. Yair is one dangerous dude and fairly high-strung. Simon and Yair are good golfers, and both are married to Anglos and speak wonderful English. Yair speaks better than any English person I have met. Yair used to take his golf seriously, and I would revel in pissing him off. Simon, I hear, is still playing Thursdays with Lulu. Lulu is another off-the-charts character, who used to play football for Hapoel Hadera.

The characters that play golf in Israel make it special. We never talked politics or the war situation. Playing golf in

Israel is like leaving the country. No matter the tragedy, golf was an escape, where you could find peace.

Fourteen

A Holy Hole in One

The second intifada started in Jerusalem on October 20.

I was technically a tourist, because I would leave the country every three months. On election night of the Bush-Gore election, I traveled to Petra in Jordan. Petra is an amazing area and home to Moses's spring. I could live in the caves of Petra and be happy. I also visited the pyramids and spent a night in Cairo, Egypt. There is still a peace agreement between both countries, and at a minimum, I hope it will continue to hold. In 1973, I obviously could not set foot in either country.

My European trips would always start in Amsterdam, and, on my first trip, I took a train across Scandinavia. Norway was the best, and its natural beauty is as pretty as anywhere in Europe. I got to cross-country ski there and had an amazing day despite horrible conditions. The people in Norway are the warmest in Scandinavia, and that is saying a lot, because Sweden and Denmark are great places. I guess I remember Vinka, an old lady friend I met back in the day in Amsterdam.

The boat ride from Bergen to Newcastle was pretty wild. We were serenaded by a Bulgarian rock band that murdered the English language with their songs. I played chess with an ex–Gaza resident. But what I remember most about that trip was the North Sea. It was fine leaving Bergen, but sometime in the middle of the night, it got rough. I spent most of my time hugging my bunk and praying we would get to Newcastle. Those crazy Norwegians never got off the boat, because they just wanted to party and buy duty-free booze.

I moved from the Park Hotel to the Carmel, which was an apartment hotel. It was much nicer and newer. The attacks that were happening seemed beyond anyone's control. If you were at the wrong place at the wrong time, you were probably dead. I kept learning and playing golf.

* * *

It was the first tournament I played in Caesarea, and by Israeli standards it was a cold and windy day. Coastal Israel has basically the same weather as Southern California. Hamadia's weather is sometimes warmer than Death Valley. The wind was at least a steady twenty-five miles per hour, with higher gusts. The tournament was full, and 144 players would attack the course that day.

The format was a two-man best-ball Stableford high score wins, with full handicap. My partner that day was Gidi; that day I barely knew him. We had played in KC a couple of times. He had a higher handicap than me and asked me to be his partner. In our group was a buddy, Laser, from Netanya, who had the right attitude about golf. His partner was his old army boss. Assaf was a retired major general and ex-chief of the national police. He is a nice-enough guy.

The front nine was a par thirty-seven with three par fives. Sometimes in golf, you fall into the zone. It had happened maybe six times in my life previous to this. At the Dos I had broken eighty twice. It didn't mean I was an eight handicap, but, if all the stars aligned, I could play good golf. That day I would score my best round ever on the old course. I was in the zone and parred three of the first four holes. Number five was a long dogleg par five and ranked the number-one handicap hole. I managed to make a long putt for bogey and a net birdie. I double-bogeyed six, but luckily, Gidi made par. I parred seven, and it was on to number eight.

The eighth hole was ranked the easiest because it was shortest hole on the course. This day the pin was tucked in its hardest position: ten meters from the edge of the bunker. The bunker had a large tree in front of it. You could see the flag but not the hole. The wind was coming in from the sea and definitely hurting. The distance was around 145 yards. I took a five iron and approached the ball; I had the honor from the last hole. In golf the honor is given to the person with the lowest score on the previous hole. The group was chattering away as I hit the ball. I pured my five iron, and it had a perfect line at the flagstick. When it came down in front of the flagstick, I felt that it went in.

When you hit a ball purely, the sound your club makes when it hits the ball is sort of a click. Maybe the group heard the sound, or maybe they felt guilty talking during my swing. The general asked me about my shot. All I could think about was that I was probably going to have to buy drinks for 144 people, and that's what I told him in Hebrew. Well, I don't think he understood, and he asked me, "Where's your ball?"

I said it was in the hole. The general must have asked the same question twenty times on the tee; and my playing partner, at least five times. Laser asked only once, but I'm sure he was laughing hard on the inside.

Everyone finished, and off we went. Gidi and I were walking; Laser and the general were riding and speeding to the green. The general gets out of the cart and screamed the same question, and I gave him the same answer. He then asked if it was OK to look in the hole. I told him please, so Laser and the general approached the hole. To their credit, they did shout for joy when they saw my ball in the hole. Gidi slapped me on the back and started to laugh. I kept a straight game face as I got to the green and walked up to the hole. When I saw the ball in the hole, I had to smile. The group was all laughing. The hole had a closest-to-the-pin contest, so I went to mark my zero distance to the pin, and since there were no zeros, I signed my name. The players finished the hole, and we started off the green. I spotted Amos and Yoram on the tee. I let out a couple of Hollis-Hills hillbilly war cries and waved.

I finished the short uphill par-five ninth with a par and broke forty for the first and only time on the front nine. I was ready to quit and never play golf again, because it had to be all downhill from the way I was feeling. There was a long wait to get off of ten, and Amos and Yoram showed up. We laughed, and the general told them the story. We had a lot of Stableford points. With my handicap, I had a zero on number eight for a net double eagle—that's five points. We had twenty-nine points going into the back nine.

I played well on the back, but not like the front, and shot forty-six for an eighty-five. We finished tied for first. In Caesarea, there are no play-offs. The first tiebreaker is the back nine, and the other team had a better back nine, so we were awarded second place. I did win a cheesy clock for closest to the pin. Since it was a tournament, there was food and an open bar. Most Jews I know are not heavy drinkers, but I was off the hook. I did ask Yoram if I could buy him a drink, and he gave me his order. I got it and served it with a smile. There was a trophy-presentation ceremony, and I got my first Caesarea trophy. The club wanted pictures, and one of them is on the cover of this book. I posed on the eighteenth green. One of the club's sponsors was *Cigar* magazine, and I was in the next issue. I was told I made the Netanya paper, but I never saw the story.

All of a sudden, a lot of people wanted to meet the nutcase from Colorado. The lady golfers of Caesarea were always fun to flirt with. There was Inez and Veronique from France and ladies from Belgium, Switzerland, Northern Ireland, England, South Africa, and Canada. My favorites from Israel were Sara, Ruti, and Penny. Aviva was actually my closest friend out of all the ladies. A lot of people didn't like Aviva, because she never lacked an opinion. She reminded me of my oldest sister. I'm sure she was a California babe in her prime. She met her husband at UCLA and married into one of the wealthier Israeli families. We would play a lot together, along with her two dentist buddies, Chuck and Clive from Haifa.

One day Simon and I were hanging out at the nineteenth hole, when I spotted some Israeli golfing babes. Simon proceeded to tell me that they would eat me for lunch and spit me out before dinner. I left them alone. The best female Israeli golfer is now a senior at the University of Florida and plays for the golf team. Back then she was a little kid. Her mom is a good buddy of Yoram. I played with her when she was little, and she was way better than her mom. She would get better and better and no doubt is the best golfer to ever come out of Israel.

My name showed up in the English papers. The *Post* now had competition, thank goodness. *Ha Aretz* is a much better paper. Jules wrote the piece about the tournament, and the same story appeared in both papers. I had my first hole in one, which wasn't true, and the tone of the story was not very friendly. I asked Jules about it, and he sort of grumbled to leave him alone. Jules was Jules. I felt like it was a holy hole in one because, the way the wind was blowing that day, it took a higher being to get it in the hole. I really felt it go in, and I thought that God had let me know it was in the hole. I knew I had fallen in love with the game of golf.

It was time to leave the country again, and I traveled to Portugal and played. I visited Bilbao and played on the Atlantic coast of Spain. I played in Bordeaux and Normandy. The course in Entretat is one of my world favorites.

I now had some buddies from Belgium and heard of some courses I should check out. Ooudenarde had the coolest clubhouse I ever visited. It was like a small castle that had a chapel where you could pray before you played. The most fun I had was in a town called Knock (pronounced with a hard *K*). My grandma used to call me a knocker when I cheated at poker. I always gave her back her pennies. In Yiddish, *knocker* means big shot.

Clervoux is not far from Battle of the Bulge country. It has a pretty course, and I did visit Bastogne and the memorials there. In Holland, Nordeweg was my favorite. In spring the fields turn into a riot of color. They used to play the Dutch Open there. The course is located on the coast, and, of course, the day I visited, the wind was blowing hard. I shot fifty-five on the front nine, which was into the wind; and forty-three on the back, which was downwind. When I went into the clubhouse for a beer after the round, I was told to remove my hat. You've got to love the Dutch.

I had been to Amsterdam on a New Year's Eve, and the city exploded at midnight with fireworks. I bought my clubs there, at Nevada Bobs. The putter I bought had a distinctive sound when it made contact with the ball because of its titanium face. Yair would call it my fucking Dutch putter. It was time to get back to Israel.

My daughters were coming to visit Israel that summer. Israel was not at war, but it was still under attack. My friends who lived in Jerusalem were falling asleep to gunfire. The suburb of Gilo came under fire from the town of Bethlehem. The coming Christmas would be canceled at the Church of the Nativity. People continued to die.

Fifteen
September 11, 2001

I was still staying at the Carmel but had started learning Arabic at the Ulpan. The kids were coming, and I needed to throw them a party in Hamadia. I thought that maybe a hundred people might show up. It would be an evening affair in the new park, and plans were made.

Some parents might think it wrong to allow my kids to come visit me in a war zone. I kept thinking it might calm down. I had been through a war, and technically Israel wasn't at war with anyone. In hindsight, I should not have allowed the visit.

Seeing the kids was great, and when we got back from the airport, we headed to the pool. We were sunning and swimming when we heard a muffled explosion. Someone turned on a radio. Some military helicopters showed up in the sky, but no suspect was picked up. A bomb had gone off outside a school on the other side of town. No one was hurt, if I remember correctly. Welcome to Netanya, girls.

The next day we had a wedding in Tel Aviv at the Dan Panorama Hotel. The oldest daughter of my old buddy from Ramle was getting married. On the way there, we passed a nightclub called the Dolphinarium, and the girls remarked on it. The next night we were in Tiberius. I was hosting the daughters of my buddy from Karkur, and they would hang out with us and attend the party the next day.

Around one in the morning, I heard strange noises coming from the room next door. I got up and listened closely, and my neighbor was screaming *why*, and I could hear the TV on. I flipped on the TV and immediately understood his anguish. Someone had blown himself up at the Dolphinarium, and it sounded like twenty-plus kids were dead. So much for the party to be held later that day. The butchery of the Middle East can be beyond description. It reminded me of another event that happened in Maalot in 1974. The Dolphinarium bombing brought Tel Aviv up in the body count and Israel to a new level of depression.

The next day I told the girls about it. Boaz grew up in Hamadia and is Arieh's oldest son. Aside from playing basketball with him when he was a kid, Boaz had visited Colorado. I got him a job at the ranch, and Boaz was a cowboy for a little while. He is a good friend. His daughters took the news in stride; people dying was not exactly new news. My girls were a little taken aback by their reaction. My girls wanted to hear about it on television. Boaz's girls were more into their teen magazines. We hit the pool and tried to forget about it.

It got to 110 degrees Fahrenheit that day, but it did cool off that evening. I didn't expect a lot of folks were going to show up, but surprisingly a good number of Hamadia folks did. I sent the DJ home, as no one felt like dancing. We ate and talked and tried to be positive with each other. The *gan* (Hebrew for garden) was beautiful, and I think the guests enjoyed themselves. Uri and Evi from Kfar Yedidiya, friends of my brother-in-law, were the only guests who made the trip from the coast. The girls got some attention, and I think they came away with a positive feeling toward Hamadia's people.

The next day we traveled south, down to the Dead Sea. We drove the length of the West Bank and past Jericho without stopping. Traveling down that road might not have been the smartest of decisions with the kids. The kids were troopers and had no fear. You can't let fear or paranoia govern your life. There had been attacks on that road, and innocent people had been killed for no reason at all. My youngest slept through most of the ride. My oldest kept me company and enjoyed the beautiful scenery.

We hung out a couple of nights on the Dead Sea. We hiked up to some waterfalls in En Gedi. We took the cable car up Messada. It was not my first trip to these places. We met very few tourists on our trip. Tourism was almost completely dead in Israel at the moment. We floated on top of the Dead Sea. We took a different route back to Netanya.

I played in the club championship in Caesarea, and my kids hung out and watched me get another trophy. I heard about a cease-fire in Jerusalem, and we went and stayed there for a couple of days. There is no city in the world like Jerusalem, and, yes, on occasions it has a golden light.

We had lunch on the porch of the King David Hotel, and the latkes were great. We walked from there into the old city. We came in from Jaffa Gate and were immediately stopped by the border police, who suggested we should not enter, because tensions were so high. I told them I just wanted to show the girls the Western Wall, and they suggested we take a cab to the Dung gate. So that's what we did, and my girls got to see the wall. We were not allowed up on the Temple Mount. We took a cab up the Mount of Olives, and the girls got to see the spot where the new messiah will rise and save the world. As we left town, the cease-fire was over, and Jerusalem would continue under siege.

The girls had a great visit for their first time in Israel. They got to meet lots of people and saw a good bit of the country. Because of their mom, I never pushed religion on them. To experience Jewish culture was new to them, and I think they saw enough religion to question it all. They would visit Israel a couple more times under less stressful conditions.

The country now had security everywhere, including in all public places. Israelis were checked before entering any public buildings: banks, restaurants, hotels, shopping centers, and the post office. I was getting antsy. I still had no plan about where I wanted to settle. Bucky and Orna now lived in Udim, and I started to think that Israel needed another golf course. I thought it should be built in Hamadia. Bucky was negative about it. The kibbutz was about to go under financially and, therefore, could not be a viable partner. Because of the land issues to be resolved, he thought it was a bad idea.

On September 11, 2001, I played a round of golf with Chuck and Clive. They played a complicated form of Bingo Bango Bongo, where you got ticks on each hole, each tick was worth a shekel, and the person with the fewest ticks had to pay the others. We had just finished our round, and Chuck was figuring out the damages. Someone was running up the first fairway looking agitated and messing with his phone. He shouted out that someone had flown into the World Trade Center, and we all headed inside.

The restaurant had a member's-only room with a TV. Sure enough, the North Tower was on fire. They weren't sure what kind of aircraft had flown into it. I didn't want to watch. It sounded like a bad deal, and that there was going to be a lot of carnage. We sat down in the restaurant and started drinking. Then a person came out of the room and told us another plane had hit the other tower. Well, everyone then knew terrorists had attacked New York City. I was kind of in shock. I was sure I knew someone who was down there, and I knew the world was about to change.

There was a feeling of hope that America would understand Israel a little better and maybe fight terrorism. I left the bar after the report of another plane hitting the Pentagon. I would go home to watch the towers crumble again and again. It was a sad evening.

When people ask me where I am from, I always say Colorado. It's where my kids live, and I have spent more time there than anyplace else. When 9-11 happened, I strangely felt like a New Yorker. My family still lived in New York, and, although they were dysfunctional, I was sure they were safe, as none of them lived or worked downtown. My younger sister, Sandy, was supposed to be in Netanya. Uri and Evi's son was to get married on the twelfth, and, of course, they were invited. They were too afraid to come to Israel because of the situation.

Indeed the headline the next day in one of Israel's largest dailies was "Don't You Feel Safe Living in Israel?" Israeli reaction, both Jewish and Arab, to 9-11 bothered me. The Arabs gave out free candy and celebrated. How people could celebrate the loss of so many innocent lives is beyond comprehension. America does not and never has understood the Middle East. Americans can't understand people who have no regard for human life. Israelis thought 9-11 would bring America closer to Israel and its fight against terror. Instead it brought overreaction and regime change in Afghanistan and Iraq. A war on terror? Hardly; it made Iran stronger and more powerful.

The intifada started when Ariel Sharon visited the Temple Mount, but Bill Clinton caused it. Bill Clinton had good intentions but could not get a peace deal done. I know he balanced the budget and brought about an economic boom in America. He was, in fact, the worst American president for Israel since Eisenhower. Old Bill thought he could bring peace to Israel. Maybe he could have succeeded if he understood the Middle East. Old Bill had a deadline, and Arafat could not agree to peace, no matter what it cost Israel. The intifada was the Palestinian reaction to the frustrating pressure that Clinton had applied during the process. America will always be hated in the Arab world, because it has been a friend to Israel. No matter the policy in the future, America will always be guilty by association.

The government of Israel fell after a year of the intifada. Ariel Sharon would take charge of the government. The change in government would take a little time, but eventually the government would crack down on the Arabs. The intifada would continue on well after 9-11. George W. Bush would be a friend to Israel. Although George W. really didn't understand the Arabs either, he gave Israel political support throughout his two terms in office. George W.'s reaction to 9-11 caused America to pay a huge price for a very limited result. The war on terrorism was not waged against the state sponsors of terrorism: Syria, Iran, and Lebanon. Al-Qaeda was the biggest threat to America? It is sad to say, but terrorists are stronger today than they were at the time of 9-11. The reason being that America's greatest enemy was Al Qaeda not the state sponsors of terrorism Syria and Iran. Our president today does not understand the Middle East either. The jury is out, and Obama has made some promises, but I have my doubts that Israel's situation will improve in the future.

I was unhappy after 9-11, and I knew a lot more people were going to die. I couldn't shake my feelings about New York. I wanted to hug my kids. September 11 changed nothing in Israel, and it would only get worse. I still hadn't found a situation I could live with in Israel. The violence in Israel I could live with if I was forced to, but I needed something to do. It was time for another trip.

Sixteen

Passover 2002

When I got back to New York in the middle of October, it seemed like a different place. New Yorkers had realized how vulnerable they were. Aside from the terror of 9-11, there were also anthrax attacks. When I went downtown to see the ruins, the whole area stunk. It wasn't a pleasant smell, and it wasn't a normal smell. The neighborhood, which was once vibrant, seemed like a ghost town.

I decided to look up Big Ed—I check in with him once a decade. Big Ed works near Chinatown, around Bowery and

Canal. He told me one of our old friends was working across the street from the towers when the planes hit. He walked to Big Ed's place in shock and covered in crap. Big Ed said he took care of him.

New Yorkers have a reputation of being tough, cold, and arrogant. I never saw any sign of those New Yorkers when I visited a month after 9-11. People were considerate of each other. I heard "Have a nice day" often, as well as "Thank you." It was obvious the city had undergone major trauma. Everyone had a story, and everyone had felt a different kind of pain. Everyone knew someone who had been there or was affected.

My family had their own stories. September 11 hadn't changed the relationship between my two sisters. They didn't speak to each other, and hadn't for twenty-plus years. My mom's death did not help their relationship, and I had given up on my relationships with both of them. Sandy would not give up on me, and we met for lunch. She had watched the towers crumble at her son's apartment when the event happened.

New York will always be a sad place for me. I have painful memories about my family there. I had to see it, though, and I could relate to the pain. It would take time, as it always does when you experience major trauma.

When I got to Colorado, I did get to hug my kids. I also heard a different perspective: "Those Arabs should've finished the job and wiped out the whole city." I couldn't believe a friend would say that, but I understood the sentiment. I don't think he had ever been to New York City in his life.

I retreated to Whistling Streams and felt empty. As beautiful and peaceful as Colorado is, I still had ghosts there too. I would try and work out of Denver. I got an insurance license and started selling health insurance. I absolutely hated it. It's hard to feel like you're helping people when you're ripping them off. I wasn't happy because I could not find my niche, and I still wanted to live in Israel.

I was supposed to land the day before the Passover holiday, but I must have read the calendar wrong. I landed on the day of the holiday. I called Bucky and was invited to dinner. I got to meet Orna's family for the first time, and Bucky's family was in full attendance.

Passover is a family holiday; Jewish tradition dictates celebration of the Seder meal. I am not a fan of the long recitation of the entire Haggadah. As a kid, I would have to go to my uncle's house, and it was a two-hour deal. Well, at Bucky's, we hit the highlights and sang a few songs. It was over quick.

Yoav and I decided to step outside. Udim is on the coastal highway, just south of Netanya. We heard the sound of sirens. Not one but many. Yoav said there must have been an attack. I figured it was time to go inside. We heard some more sirens, but no one wanted to speculate on what might have happened. After dinner I got to the Carmel, and I knew the lady behind the desk. She had tears in her eyes and asked me if I knew what had happened.

A bomb had gone off in the Park Hotel, killing a lot of people. We both knew people who worked there. Hell, I knew the owners. I asked about the person who lived on the sixth floor, but she didn't know. I went up to my room heartsick. I knew people who might have been killed.

The Park bombing killed almost thirty people, mostly Swedes celebrating the holiday there. It would trigger a call-up of some reserves and the clampdown on many Palestinian towns and cities. It was the beginning of the end of the Palestinian uprising. The government decided to build a security fence, and there would still be another year of violence, but no doubt security would get stronger and stronger.

Ami was a nice guy who had married the daughter of the owners of the Park Hotel. He had ten kids and no desire to die. Netanya was a frequent target for the bombers of the intifada. I don't want to list all the incidents of attack and loss of life that happened in Netanya during the intifada. There were many, and Ami decided to wear a pistol at work. When a bomber walked out of the kitchen and blew himself up, it didn't matter that Ami was armed, because it happened before he knew it. He didn't die at the scene, but, a couple of days later, he was gone.

I went to the golf course the next morning, and, like always, passed the Park Hotel. The international press was gathered and doing their job. I looked inside and saw people mopping up the blood. If anyone remembers seeing me that day, I was not my normal self. I wanted the attacks to end and felt the West Bank needed to be reoccupied. That was about to happen, but it should have happened months earlier. Israel had shown amazing restraint, but it was finally time to act. Districts A, B, and C would be treated the same, and the occupation would return to the harshness of the past.

To me, the people of Netanya are heroes. What they endured and how they endured it showed me strength and courage. Netanya is no longer the small town I watched my sister get married in. A forest of apartment buildings now surrounds my brother-in-law's house, where I listened to man land on the moon. Every Saturday night people walk the main street and sit in the square of cafés. People dance and celebrate life in Netanya.

One day I was walking into town when what I thought was a sonic boom occurred. It rattled windows. When I got to the square, people were running in every direction. When I asked one person what was going on, he said, "*Pigua*," (Hebrew for terror attack) and took off. I walked over to a bank and asked the security guard what he thought had happened, and he thought the Pizza Hut had been bombed. It didn't sound right to me, and I asked another person and got a different story. The result of what was going on was that the streets had emptied. I figured it was time to head home. When I passed a car-rental place with the radio on, I asked what was going on. He said there was no specific attack confirmed, but an investigation was under way. It was a sonic boom. The city of Netanya was shell-shocked.

The intifada was now at its peak. I wanted to be in Hamadia, and the more I thought about it, a golf course made sense. Bucky was still of the opinion that I shouldn't get involved there. Yoav ran Hamadia and was Bucky's brother, and he thought it was a great idea. He didn't know that I knew about their financial mess. Times were tough, but Hamadia was hanging on.

Then my friend Gidi came up with an idea for me to sell granite for him in the States. Gidi has a beautiful house in Caesarea. He thought I could help him and make money. Gidi represented Caesarstone, which was produced at Kibbutz Sdot Yam, which borders Caesarea. He also represented a kibbutz up north that sold natural granite.

There was also a factory in Nazareth that competed against Caesarstone. That is the product I would focus on. Gidi and I were in Denver and called on a few accounts. Gidi went back to Israel but gave me samples and told me to find some business. I went and talked to a major granite distributor that had more than one location. His business was growing, and I was talking about an exclusive product line. I would take an office in his building and help market the product. They agreed to commit to a test, and, following its successful conclusion, they would make a multi-million-dollar commitment. I went back to Israel and saw Gidi, and we took a trip to the factory in Nazareth. The factory looked forward to the new business. Gidi was positive he would get it worked out, and I went back to Denver.

A day after I got back, Gidi was a completely different person. He spouted incredible nonsense, but the bottom line was that he wanted me to send back his samples and leave him alone. I guess he thought he could steal the deal from me. I know he tried. Maybe he had a contract conflict. Who knows? I knew I had to tell a Denver company the truth.

My hole-in-one witness had slimed me big-time. When I build my course, he is banned from playing there. Whether the stories he told me about himself are true doesn't matter. He caused me major embarrassment, and I will never speak to him again.

When the Jewish Olympics happened, security finally came to Caesarea. There were snipers on top of the clubhouse to protect thirty foreign golfers. Because of the situation, not as many athletes would show up for the Maccabiah Games. Having so few contestants, the golf club decided to have a Maccabiah tournament for its members, and I won my last trophy. The presentation ceremony was at the Tel Aviv

Hilton. Bucky let me take Orna to the event. I think there were at least five hundred people there. Pomp and Circumstance, the Ethiopian dancers, were the highlight. Orna got some parting gifts. When they called me up to collect my trophy, the corporate dude gave me the wrong one. I rolled with it and got the right one later. It was a good party.

It's sad that, every Yom Kippur, I think about all the people who died that day in 1973. Now, every Passover, I think about the people who died at the Park Hotel in 2002. The miracle of the state of Israel requires sacrifice. Some day a generation will be born that won't have to kill to ensure its survival. I doubt I will live long enough to see that.

Seventeen

Golf Heaven

Zev, Yonkale, Simon, and Yair, "The Boys at Spanish Bay"

It just wasn't happening for me in Israel. I could not find a comfortable situation for myself. Being mostly self-employed and over fifty limited my options. I moped back to Colorado again. I tried selling windows and siding, and that was miserable work. Eventually I finally sold my house in Whistling Streams and decided to go someplace totally new: California.

Of course I knew California from many previous visits and decided to move to golf heaven. I landed in Pacific Grove and decided to get a real-estate license. Pacific Grove separates Monterey from Pebble Beach. It sits off Monterey Bay and extends almost to Spanish Bay. Its coastline makes it one of the prettiest places on the planet.

There are many golf courses in and around the Pacific Grove area, and it is difficult to decide where to play. Pacific Grove, Rancho Canada, Bayonet, Blackhorse, Del Monte, Spanish Bay, Poppy Hills, Spyglass, and Pebble Beach were some of the places to choose from. Pacific Grove (PG) was my home course, and it was the most affordable—and a resident got an even better deal.

The PG course is the ultimate grandpa course, as it is not long (that plus the back nine plays along the Pacific Ocean). Simon never liked the PG course, because the first two holes bordered a graveyard. Simon, Yonkale, and Yair were members of Caesarea who came to visit in the area. We all played Spanish Bay together. Of the Pebble Beach–owned courses, Spanish Bay is my favorite. That day, Yonkale and I would find almost a hundred golf balls. Somewhere in the poop on eighteen lies an eight iron of mine. Having a Caesarea foursome in Pebble Beach was a lot of fun. Yonkale caddied for me in a senior match-play deal in PG. I think he liked my opponent better than he liked me, and, by the back nine, he was giving me a hard time. I still won in spite of Yonkale.

California is like a world unto itself, and agriculturally it can grow absolutely anything. Its light, especially around sunsets, is special. You can get lost in California—or suffocated. It is not an inexpensive place to live. Taxes are high, and there are many of them. A lot of people have the Hollywood dream. When I was there, the real-estate boom was getting close to its peak.

I entered the Prudential training program and began studying for my license test. There I met the ninja lady, who was a recent transplant, and we became friends. She was taking the test too and was in the program. She had been through a divorce and tough times. One of her hobbies was Japanese sword-fighting. She really was a ninja. She liked photography and wasn't bad at it. She had a twinkle in her eye, and she was no dummy. I wanted to go around the world together, but at the time she wasn't ready. Years later she said she was ready and then disappeared.

The ninja lady and I passed the test the first time and got our licenses. The California test is supposed to be the hardest, and 50 percent fail the first time they take it. We both worked for Prudential in Carmel, in an office of mostly women and run by a woman. I found almost no marketing support, and I realized I had to build my own customer base. (Not easy for a new kid in town.) The ninja lady had the same problem.

The market wasn't a problem. Money for mortgages was easily obtainable, and one could borrow a lot and pay very little. On a variable-rate thirty-year loan, one could borrow five hundred thousand dollars and pay as little as eight hundred a month. We all know that the bubble burst in 2008. Back then, if a property was reasonably priced, it would receive multiple offers beyond its asking price. It was a seller's market.

I knew it would take time, and just because I had a license did not mean I would make money. The business was a lot harder than I had thought. I was frustrated with the Carmel office and found a Pacific Grove company willing to take me in. It was a walk to the office, and the office was selling property.

My neighbors were a couple with kids in an apartment that was too small for them. I talked them into prequalifying for a mortgage. He qualified for a $350,000 loan, and that meant he could not afford anything in the immediate area. Hollister, about twenty-five miles away, became an option. I made a few trips and studied the market. I recommended a three-bedroom condo on the golf course. My neighbor wasn't sure, and there was not a lot of property on the market in his price range. Then out of the blue, he decided to go to Hollister on his own, looked at my recommendation, and decided to buy. The listing agent said that if he brought in his own realtor, he would not get the property, so my neighbor took the deal and screwed me out of a commission. Welcome to California real estate.

My office had listings, and its hottest properties were out by the Bayonet and Blackhorse golf courses. It was a KB homes subdivision, and the owner of the company had bought several homes and flipped them successfully. I learned that if you work an open house and sell the property, you get paid absolutely nothing. The real-estate market can be extremely cutthroat, and you have to pay your dues. The ninja lady had no sales and left one office and went to another. She enjoyed having family in the area, at least.

I thought my breakthrough would come from my home course. I used to play regularly with three grandpas, and they were always supportive. They also knew how to laugh. Mr. Watt was from England. Pickle was always giving Lizard a hard time, just like Yonkale and Amos. I met some wonderful people during my time in golf heaven.

There are vast swaths of coastal California that are still wild and undeveloped. The Point Reyes National Seashore borders

Bolinas, though it is best accessed from Olema. Coastal sunsets are special. Big Sur was closer to home, but the conditions had to be right. The Smith River above Crescent City and the Trinity River below are incredible areas. It's hard to feel blue when you live with beautiful nature. The farther north in California you go, the wetter it gets, and sometimes a blue-sky day becomes rare. If the state of Jefferson ever came into being, California could get rid of its cloudier coastline.

Real estate was frustrating for me. The market was hot, and people were making money. I didn't know a lot of people, but I was meeting a lot people playing golf. It is not cheap living in California, and I needed to produce an income for myself.

In Israel, the intifada was finally over.

I really do love golf. Playing so many beautiful courses inspired me. Poppy Hills is home to the Northern California Golf Association. It is everything a golf course should be. At Poppy there are equal amounts of par fives, fours, and threes. Although the topography of Hamadia is much different, the course I have designed is similar to the concept of Poppy. I just hope mine can be maintained as well as Poppy's.

Pacific Grove is a great, affordable course despite being shortish. The Pebble courses are resort-style courses. Spyglass was the longest and always pure torture for me. Spanish Bay was more my speed but a challenge. I still wonder if anyone ever found my eight iron. I got to play Pebble Beach a couple of times. Some people call Pebble one of the high cathedrals of golf. It does have drama, but, compared to Spyglass and Spanish Bay, it is easier. Of course Pebble has outstanding ocean holes and a few very difficult holes. I managed to score well there compared to Spyglass or Spanish Bay. Del Monte is in Monterey and was also run by the Pebble Beach Company. It is another challenging layout, but not as pretty as the other Pebble courses. Being a Duke member gets you a deal at all four places.

The Bayonet and Blackhorse courses were once part of Fort Ord. Both are fantastic courses. It is said the general in charge liked to fade the ball, and so the courses were designed accordingly. I'm not sure if that's true, but I like to fade the ball because it is easier to hit than a draw. The Bayonet is longer, but the Blackhorse is more fun. Both are well maintained and affordable with a membership card—definitely a better deal than the Pebble courses.

Rancho Canada is in the Carmel Valley and is a public course that I enjoyed playing on. As you enter the course, there is a sign that reads, "Pray," with an arrow pointed in one direction, and, "Play," with an arrow pointed in another direction. Like in Ooudenarde, I think it's always a good idea to pray before you play. Carmel and Pebble have quite a few private courses, but I haven't heard of any with prayer chapels.

It was tough deciding where to play. I started to think I wanted to build a course for myself. I had a partner in Hamadia, even if bankruptcy loomed. Surely a great venture could survive. The new venture would be separate from the kibbutz. Golf didn't have to be expensive to build, especially with the existing water structure there. Why not live your dream?

This was an Independence Day skit in Hamadia. Even though the girls were beating me up, Hamadia residents loved the idea.

The kids loved the idea too, and always wanted to learn.

Eighteen
Jordan River Golf

The aerial view of the National Park and golf-course site from a hang glider.

Golf heaven was good for my golf game, and my home-course handicap dropped to an all-time low of fourteen. Pacific Grove is not the most difficult course, but I was also playing a lot more difficult courses. It is true that the more you play, the better you get.

When I decided to try and build a golf course, I tried to organize the process. The first thing was to get Hamadia's formal approval. I called Bucky's brother Yoav, and he was supportive. When we talked about the money to build the course, he was concerned, because Hamadia had no money to contribute to the process. It did have the land. Yoav wanted me to prove I could raise the money, before we went to the local authorities to gain their blessing.

That was reasonable, and I began drawing up a business plan. Israelis may not understand golf, but they do understand business. I drew up a conservative plan based on the existing golfers in Israel. I knew the Caesarea Club well, and I had real numbers. Golf development, such as a resort and housing, takes bigger money to do, but it also generates more revenue. Most people thought golf could not make money as a stand-alone business. I used Caesarea and a few American models to show otherwise.

A few people have tried to build golf courses in Israel. My good American friend from Caesarea has been trying for twenty-five years and has never been successful. Richard is not only a better golfer than I am, but also he is smarter and has a formal education and degrees. Richard has proposed golf courses in many places, mostly kibbutzim and moshavim. Richard is a certified and licensed architect. He was also professor at a Tel Aviv university. Richard never lived on a kibbutz or a moshav and does not enjoy speaking

Hebrew. He helped me with some technical aspects of my business plan. Richard is fun to play golf with, and I would love to see him succeed.

Another project was supposed to be built near Ashkelon by South African developers. They had the government approvals and started building houses. They made so much money building houses, they forgot about building the golf course.

A Florida real-estate mogul conceived yet another project. His idea was to build a luxury golf course community and resort above Tiberius. A friend of mine was his front man, and he received government approvals. He wasted an incredible amount of money. With the money he wasted, I could have built three golf courses, and his project remains a colossal failure.

Once my business plan was written, it was time to address Yoav's concern about money. I Googled golf-development investors and made several inquiries. One company out of Luxembourg was genuinely interested. I spoke with the principal, and he said he had heard of Hamadia and asked for a contact number. I gave him Yoav's number, but I doubted he ever heard of Hamadia. He spoke with Yoav and told him he was ready to put millions in a golf-development project with Hamadia. There was a catch, of course, and that was that he wanted me out of the project. Now Yoav may have doubted the viability of the golf project, but he could no longer doubt my ability to find money for the project. Yoav and I have known each other for many years; he was a guest of mine when I was living in New York, once upon a time. I was a good friend of his brother's. Yoav knew he could trust me. The kibbutz was getting closer to filing for bankruptcy. Yoav turned down the company's offer.

I contacted a large number of golf-course builders, famous and not-so-famous, and asked about their interest in building an affordable golf course in Israel. A few responded, and one showed real interest. He confirmed that a course could be built there for a reasonable amount of money, and he wanted to take on the project. I was honest about the problems I faced, and he offered to help me in any way possible.

I decided to build a website, and that the proper name for the course would be the Jordan River Golf Club. I designed a logo, which I thought represented a sunrise over the Bashan Hills. It was time to go back to Hamadia and confirm plans with Yoav.

When I got back to Israel, I visited Bucky first and was hoping for his help and support. To my surprise, he liked the website and business plan. He knew I had spent some time and money, and that proved I was serious. I respected Bucky a lot and knew he was no dummy when it came to business. He had a degree in economics from the Hebrew university in Jerusalem, and his last job before leaving the kibbutz was as a bank president. The kibbutz bank was owned by the movement and was run for the benefit of the many kibbutzes all over the country. Bucky still loved Hamadia, and, although he knew next to nothing about golf, he wanted to help.

When I visited Yoav, he too liked the business plan and website. The kibbutz formally accepted the plan, and Yoav and I visited the local authorities. They were supportive and wanted more details. Yoav suggested I move back to Hamadia and get busy. I had some loose ends to tie up before I could move in. Before I left, I met with an old friend who used to live in Hamadia. Moran was a civil engineer, and, like me, had once upon a time worked for Mordi. He liked the idea of the project and would give me a deal on the surveying. He also recommended a master planner. Avishai seemed a gentle soul with tons of experience in all types of building projects. I asked the director of business development for the local government about him. The director had worked with him on many occasions and praised him highly. That worked for me, and I paid Avishai a retainer for his future work.

Yoav and I agreed the site for the course should be surrounding the new national park. There are prettier places in Hamadia, but none had the accessibility of the park. The park site also had the advantage of not requiring a land-use change. The park was already zoned for tourism business, and I could locate the business of golf (the clubhouse) within the park. The course would surround the park on agricultural land. It was essential to me that the farmland retained its agricultural status. I had plans to surround the course with date and olive trees. I also wanted to build a couple of ponds that could be used in conjunction with Hamadia's fish-farming operation. It is important for any golf course to have cost-effective water available. Being agricultural means that the water the land uses is for agricultural purposes and is therefore charged the lowest possible rate. You may argue that golf is not agriculture, but you cannot argue that a golf course is not maintained as carefully as is farmland.

I had to leave again but would be back soon. Moran would start the survey work in my absence. I had made important progress. The kibbutz and the local government supported the idea of bringing golf to the Bet Shean Valley.

Many people in Israel believed it was impossible to do business with a kibbutz. My buddy Richard had many more nightmares than I had. I am sure if Hamadia was like it used to be, it would have made it a lot easier for me. I wanted to build a golf course, because I love the game of golf. Because of the situation of golf in Israel, the sport really needs an affordable golf course. I was doing this not to become rich, but because I love golf, and I love Hamadia. Yes, there would be an opportunity to make a lot of money in a resort and housing, but that was not my focus. Once the golf course was built, I could think about that. The resort and housing would have far less value without a golf course.

While I was back in the States, Moran completed the survey work, and I wired him payment. When I got back to Israel, Moran was first on the list to visit. When Moran showed me the survey map he had prepared, my heart sank. He did not do the survey work on the ground I had asked for. Evidently Halootz, who was in charge of building within the kibbutz, paid Moran a visit when he began to work. Halootz didn't like the idea that a small portion of the course would be on prime farmland. He steered Moran in the wrong direction, and Moran listened to him rather than the person who was paying his bill. Not exactly a simple survey job.

Moran eventually got it right, and, yes, it cost me more money. Now it was Avishai's turn. He had to take Moran's survey map and turn it into a site plan for the local government. I decided to draw the routing plan for the golf course. I wasn't building a golf course in America, and Avishai knew nothing about golf. Asking my American builder to come to Israel to do it didn't make economic sense. I doubt anyone in Israel had seen a routing plan for a golf course, and I assumed (correctly) that it was no big deal. My American builder was not going to be a factor in my obtaining the approvals I needed. He was nice enough to tell me the proper dimensions for routing a hole.

I called my buddy in Karkur and asked if he had a long tape measure. Boaz was in the real-estate business and had a fifty-meter-long tape. I told him what I was up to and asked if he wanted to help. He agreed and eventually, together, we double-checked the dimensions of Moran's survey work. I might not be a professional golf architect, but I wanted to be sure a real golf course would fit on the land I had chosen. Boaz's mom and dad still live in Hamadia and are among my closest friends. Boaz did not play golf yet, but he wanted to learn. He loved my idea to build a course around the park. I now could vision the course I wanted to build. I drew the map accordingly and gave Avishai the final piece he needed for the site plan.

I had settled in Hamadia, and all was well. The intifada was a thing of the past, and I was living in a community with many old friends. I still escaped regularly to Caesarea. When Avishai called and said the site plan was complete, it was time again to meet with the local government.

Mike not only was in charge of business development but also was in charge of planning for the local government. Mike is the son of a rabbi and grew up in one of the five towns on the south shore of Long Island, New York. Mike is religious, lives in Kibbutz Tiriat Zvi, and is someone I like very much. Mike saw no problem with the site plan. The next step was a lot more complicated and involved the Israel Lands Administration (*Minhal* in Hebrew).

I needed a lawyer, and so I asked my good buddy Simon for a recommendation. There is no shortage of lawyers who play golf at Caesarea. Simon was skeptical about my getting involved with Hamadia. He had sold one of Hamadia's factories and was having a tough time getting paid. He recommended Kobe, and that would prove to be an extremely wise choice. Kobe loves golf and wants Israel to have more golf courses. Israel can be an extremely small place. Everyone knows someone who knows the same person. In this case, Kobe turned out to be Bucky's lawyer and represented the whole family in some land that Grandma had left the family. Bucky naturally thought Simon's recommendation a good one.

But before any meaningful work could begin with Kobe, the whole situation changed. The event I had been warned about happened. Hamadia had to file for bankruptcy protection. The electric company could no longer tolerate nonpayment of funds, and it was turning off the power a few hours a day. The kibbutz charged its members for electricity, but the money went someplace else. It wasn't the only thing the kibbutz mishandled for its members. Hamadia's nightmare had begun.

Nineteen

The Journey

This view is looking toward the town of Bet Shean and the Gilboa, with a simulated course on the site.

Having a feeling of helplessness was not a new sensation for me. I had definitely been warned the bankruptcy was going to happen. I was hoping at least we could have gotten Minhal approval. Of the 140-plus members, maybe 10 percent were surprised. Some would lose their cash savings that the kibbutz held for them. Most had gotten their money out.

Once upon a time, Hamadia was a thriving community, and its members were snobs. There are no snobs that remain living in Hamadia today. What staggered me was the accumulated debt of thirty-two million dollars. The two factories were responsible for the majority of debt. Yoav had kept the place alive for as long as he could. He was blamed and bad-mouthed by many members of the collective. The truth is that every member was to blame.

The court appointed a fixer to liquidate Hamadia's assets. The court-appointed trustee was a true cowboy, and Hamadia was not his first rodeo. He did amazing work for the people who remained in Hamadia. Of course, whatever he did he would not be liked, because he was an outsider making money off their misery. The dreams of Hamadia's pioneers were officially crushed for good. They had achieved greatness, but the brutality of change overwhelmed the system. A true socialist way of life works only if the group believes in the group. In Hamadia, individuals wanted their own rewards, and the system collapsed.

I went to the local government to say good-bye to the project. The head of the local government at the time told me not to give up. She thought maybe a deal could be worked out. The Motza had partnered with several businesses, with mixed results. If you think about it, golf can be extremely successful with government participation. Pacific Grove's golf course is owned by the town. Bethpage's courses are owned by the state of New York. New York City's parks department is responsible for numerous city courses. All offer affordable golf.

A deal with the Motza was not to be, as the head of the Motza would be offered a position in the national government. Two council members, one who grew up in Hamadia, would replace her. While supporting the project, they had no desire to actually invest in it.

In Israel at this time, the warrior Ariel Sharon ran the government. Corruption was rampant, and many of his closest allies in government would be brought up on charges. One of his sons would even be convicted. The Minhal controls all real-estate development within the country. Its former head is now under indictment. I never had the money for bribes.

The court-appointed trustee and I finally met. He saw the logic in my plan. He operated on a handshake and was not excited about a written agreement but promised cooperation. He wanted me to just go ahead and build the project without Minhal approval. Indeed, it was tempting, and some successful projects have gotten away with it. Kobe said I needed a written agreement, and that eventually I would get one. It would just take time, and until I had one, the project could not move forward. I would still search for partners, but, without a written agreement on the land, the possibility was remote. The court could not be a partner in the deal.

Spinning my wheels and being patient was difficult. My friends in Hamadia had their own worries and concerns. One worry was being forced to leave their homes. Although the security situation had improved, the members who remained would be subject to the mercy of the bankruptcy court. The liquidation was under way.

Golf was the great escape and still lots of fun. Hamadia now had two golfers in residence. Spacely was from Sydney, Australia, and is a far better golfer than I am. The Space had married a lovely lady from Bet Shean.

When she became homesick, the family moved to Israel and settled in Hamadia. Space is not Jewish and did not speak much Hebrew at the time. Israel was a little overwhelming for him, but the Space is a trooper and an artist. The Space is a musician, and he survived off of various gigs. His wife studied and became a teacher. The Space obviously thought the prospect of golf in Hamadia was a great idea. I had bought a few holes and pins and had set them up in Hamadia. We would practice our short game, and we always drew a crowd of kids. We had a good time trying to teach them the basics. One day I topped a shot, and it rolled forty meters into the hole. I made Hamadia's first hole in one, and the Spaceman just shook his head and laughed.

On one Independence Day, the residents threw a party. The entertainment was a funny skit that had singing and dancing. The skit was about a new couple looking for a place to live in Hamadia. I was asked to play myself, and a group of dancers would do their thing with golf clubs I provided. The big finish of the number was their beating me up with clubs. We all had a good laugh and an enjoyable evening.

Israel has a unique political system that always seems as if it's in constant turmoil. It has around thirty political parties, and it seems like there are six new ones for every election. Keeping everyone happy is not a simple concept. When the system is corrupt, it kind of feeds upon itself. The government itself, though, can be a powerful friend.

Nitzan has an office opposite Bank Leumi in the town of Bet Shean, and we visited often. Nitzan is a kibbutznik who lives on top of the Gilboa. He represented the small business administration (MATI). His job is to promote and help small business in the Bet Shean Valley. He understood the value and positive impact of a project like mine. The bottom line was that Nitzan did everything possible. He gave me two tiny government grants. One I used, and the other I hope to use someday soon.

The first grant was for the rewriting of my business plan into Hebrew. A government-approved consultant did it. I had a choice of three and made a selection. He got the job done, and a local-government committee that included the ministry of tourism approved the plan. The Minhal approved a plan for final disposition. To receive consideration from the Minhal, they require the cash equivalent of a third of the project's value.

I had to find a partner for the project—something I had been trying to do since Hamadia's bankruptcy. Of the dozens who had shown interest, none would commit. My fancy friends in Caesarea would not help me. The Israel Golf Federation wrote a letter, which was less than a powerful endorsement. Their mission of promoting golf in Israel involved only two golf clubs. People who genuinely meant well seemed powerless to help.

In the summer of 2006, a war with Hezbollah broke out. Missiles, sometimes more than a hundred a day, would fall on northern Israel. The northern part of Israel was under attack. Israel lacked the technology and had no defense at the time. People died.

A member of Hamadia had a brother visit over the Sabbath. They hung out and had a good time at the pool. The next day the brother was driving to work in Haifa, and a missile landed close enough to force him off the road, and he died. A picture of the member at his brother's funeral was constantly shown on CNN—I guess as a symbol of Israel's grief.

In the first war with Iraq, Israel would be under missile attack. The United States did not want Israel to respond. They needed support from a coalition of countries. Israel did not respond to Iraq's missiles. In 2006 the United States wanted Israel to invade Lebanon and wipe out the Hezbollah missiles. Israel had no desire to invade Lebanon again. Its incursion at the end of the war was short-lived and accomplished nothing. Israel's air force controlled the sky and could bomb at will, but it could not stop the missile attacks.

This war would be hard on northern Israel, but the majority of Israel's population was beyond Hezbollah-missile range. Lebanon seemed under the control of Hezbollah. Hezbollah seemed under the control of Iran. The war had a limited death toll. But it put Israel on notice that Iran could make life miserable. The war came to an end with a whimper.

In Israel, sometimes the conversation will drift to the next war. Israel has no desire for more war. Its neighbors don't quite get it. For them, just to inflict pain is a victory. One day they will push too far, and we will all perish. Until a new reality can be found, a future cannot be thought about. Israel is all about living for today.

Watching Israel for over forty-four years has been a journey. I have done my best to try to create a positive situation for myself there. I have made many meaningful relationships there. I have no desire to be negative, and I try and see the best in people. Once upon a time, I wasn't sure if I would see 1974. It's all been bonus time since then.

I wish and obsess over leaving a positive legacy there. This book, if you remember, has a purpose. I cannot give up on Israel. As painful as the journey has been at times, I cannot help but want a better future there. The insanity of survival there is hard to comprehend and master.

I have tried to forget all the failures. Failing is not a pleasant experience. The best is all you can do. A little bit of luck can help a lot, but you have to make your own luck. At the end of the day, you cannot expect other people to do it for you. You can't constantly beat your head against the wall. You have to stay balanced. When life becomes unbearable for me, I become restless. Eventually that restlessness creates the need to move on.

The members of Hamadia got to keep their homes. The court would forgive huge amounts of its debt. Hamadia has a future.

Twenty
The End of the Beginning

In 2008, the signs began to point to an economic collapse, starting with the dollar's tumble in value. The housing bubble was about to burst. Times were about to become hard. I still was talking with potential investors, but deep inside, I knew it was hopeless. I was a beaten man and figured that it might be easier in America.

When you have given every effort that you can and come up short, the result can be devastating. Failure and dealing with it can be a never-ending battle. Sometimes events overwhelm you, and things happen beyond your control. When you have misjudged and made mistakes, blame is not an issue. It's all on you, and no one can relate. When you slip into the abyss, you just can't be at peace with yourself.

When you are at war with yourself, it becomes all about survival. It's one day at a time. Relationships are simple, because you limit them. You fall off the grid and wish for no contact, other than what is relevant to survive. The pain can be blocked, but it never goes away. Israel was at war in the south, the American economy was crumbling, and I was at war with myself.

Denial is a powerful escape tool in survival mode. It just never happened; the pain and frustration are not really there. When you're in the abyss, you crave solitude, and it becomes your balance. Pain management becomes a routine exercise. Making peace with yourself becomes the primary focus of your being.

It's a sad business, giving up on life—forgetting about joy and giving up on yourself. Maybe tomorrow I will figure it out and get myself moving again. Maybe tomorrow I can make something positive happen. Maybe tomorrow I will feel no pain. At the end of the day, you control your own destiny. You can deny yourself for only so long.

The truth is what you make it, and in the end, you realize all the positive forces of your being. In my case, it's been an amazing journey. I have seen and explored much beauty in the world and have made positive things happen. If I leave life tomorrow, I know I have tried my hardest to be a positive force. People I have met along the way know that. The special ones have shown me love and understanding.

We live in changing times, and not many people I know can predict the future. You cannot live in fear and denial. You can't feel sorry for yourself or correct your mistakes. Most of all, you can't give up on yourself.

Israel may some day perish and cease to exist. So what? I have had the good fortune to know and understand the meaning of its survival. I know the miracle of its existence. It may be hard for some to understand and tolerate. For me, as long as it exists, there is hope for the world.

America is also evolving and at war with itself. Time is running out for the boomers. Good times will be their legacy; and selfishness and instant gratification, their gift to the generation that follows. The corporate control over society is well under way. Freedoms are disappearing, and regular people seem powerless. We deny our mistakes and kick the can down the road. As Americans, we assume we are the greatest country in the world. Americans seem to think that's enough. Maybe tomorrow it will get better.

Our environment is also changing, and you can call it whatever you want. We are killing the planet, as well as ourselves, for the corporate good. Maybe, someday, helping the environment can be a global priority. Until then, we can hope there will be enough water next year.

The nuclear generation has created push-button warfare. Technology now dominates our lives. Could we survive if the power went off? What would we do without smart phones? The next generation will have its issues, for sure.

The natural beauty that exists in the world is under attack. Can it be saved, or must it be sacrificed for the corporate good? The beauty in our world is what makes life special. It seems to be our last refuge and hope. Thank god it still exists. It's where I need to be.

A visit by some old friends recently inspired me to become more involved in trying to fulfill my dream. The blues are still a part of my life but are under control. A plan exists now again, as do options. Life has many challenges and opportunities, and I believe I am strong enough to find my way.

Negativity is not my way, and this story has tried to avoid it as much as possible. "I am what I am," said Popeye the Sailor Man. I have played the Jordan River Golf course in my mind. I put everything I had into it and came up a little bit short. All the words I have written in this story will, I hope. change that.

Am I crazy for wanting to build a golf course in Israel? I don't think so. I hope that you can now understand why it is my obsession. Golf is more than a game; it is a way of life. In America I hear that there are twenty-three million golfers who play on several thousand golf courses. Golf has contributed to the quality of life. It has made a positive impact on many lives and enhanced the value of real estate. It is also a multi-billion-dollar-a-year industry.

Israel may be blown off the face of the earth tomorrow, but it needs an affordable golf course today. Who knows? Some day it might promote a new reality. I know it would have a positive impact on many lives.

*Redlands Mesa, Colorado National Monument.
Grand Junction, Colorado.*

www.ingramcontent.com/pod-product-compliance
Lightning Source LLC
Chambersburg PA
CBHW032256150426
43195CB00008BA/477